Blessed Are the Chosen

The
CHOSEN
An Interactive Bible Study
Season 2

Blessed Are the Chosen

Amanda Jenkins, Dallas Jenkins, & Douglas S. Huffman

DAVID C COOK
transforming lives together

BLESSED ARE THE CHOSEN
Published by David C Cook
4050 Lee Vance Drive
Colorado Springs, CO 80918 U.S.A.

Integrity Music Limited, a Division of David C Cook
Brighton, East Sussex BN1 2RE, England

The graphic circle C logo is a registered trademark of David C Cook.

ISBN 978-0-8307-8270-3
eISBN 978-0-8307-8271-0

© 2022 The Chosen, LLC

The Team: Michael Covington, Stephanie Bennett, Jack Campbell, Susan Murdock
Cover Design: James Hershberger
Interior Graphics: Getty Images (horse/cart and Ten Commandments)

Printed in the United States of America
First Edition 2022

1 2 3 4 5 6 7 8 9 10

093021

CONTENTS

Introduction

THE SERMON ON THE MOUNT

"Seeing the crowds, he [Jesus] went up on the mountain,

and when he sat down, his disciples came to him. And

he opened his mouth and taught them, saying:

Blessed are the poor in spirit, for theirs is the kingdom of heaven.

Blessed are those who mourn, for they shall be comforted.

Blessed are the meek, for they shall inherit the earth.

Blessed are those who hunger and thirst for righteousness,

for they shall be satisfied.

Blessed are the merciful, for they shall receive mercy.

Blessed are the pure in heart, for they shall see God.

Blessed are the peacemakers, for they shall be called sons of God.

Blessed are those who are persecuted for righteousness' sake,

for theirs is the kingdom of heaven.

Blessed are you when others revile you and persecute you

and utter all kinds of evil against you falsely on my account.

Rejoice and be glad, for your reward is great in heaven, for so

they persecuted the prophets who were before you."

Matthew 5:1–12

Blessed is both a familiar and unfamiliar word. Christians tend to use it in place of the word *lucky*, lest anyone think *we think* good things happen by chance. We also "bless this food to our bodies" before eating, mind our manners with a "bless you" after sneezing, give our blessing to things we like and withhold it from things we don't, and believe our judgment is subtle when we "bless his heart"—especially if we use a southern drawl.

Blest? Or bless-ED??

But in Matthew 5, Jesus used the word **nine times**, which begs the question: What does the word **blessed** really mean? And while we're at it, is it pronounced with one syllable or two?

Of course, the real issue isn't how to pronounce the twenty-first-century English word, but instead how the first-century word was defined. While most English translations of Matthew 5 use the word *blessed*, a few use the word *happy*. And indeed, happiness is included in some New Testament contexts (as in, *if you do this, you'll be happy*, like in Matt. 24:46, Luke 11:28, and Deut. 28:1–14)—but not all. In the Sermon on the Mount, the "blessed" statements are not "do this and be happy" life hacks; they aren't expressions of conditional expectation. Rather, <u>they are declarations of what already is</u> for the those who follow Jesus. Perhaps each sentence could just as easily begin with "congratulations."

The first-century Greek word for *blessed* was *makários* (μακάριος), and it's used 50 times in the New Testament.

Conditional expectation: things we have to do in order to get something in return.

Congratulations to those who are poor in spirit, because theirs is the kingdom of heaven.

Congratulations to those who mourn, because they shall be comforted.

Congratulations to those who are meek, because they shall inherit the earth.

Congratulations and so on and so forth because God's favor is upon you.

And now we're getting somewhere because as we're going to see in the coming pages, God's favor is better than happiness, contrary to the "pursue happiness no matter the cost" culture we live in. Happiness, by definition, is conditional, which means it's also temporary and most often fleeting. On the contrary, the blessings Jesus spoke of—usually called the Beatitudes—point to a fuller, more significant kind of human flourishing. Not in the material sense like those who seem to "have it all," but in the faith-affirming, peace-abiding, future-securing sense our souls truly long for.

Beatitudes: the blessings listed by Jesus in the Sermon on the Mount.

So who gets to experience God's favor? Well, only those who follow Jesus.

In our season 1 Bible study called *What Does It Mean to Be Chosen?* we focused on Isaiah 43, the Old Testament anticipation of a coming Messiah, and what the arrival of Jesus meant and still means for His followers. Specifically, we explored what it means to be called and rescued by Jesus, to rest in His presence, to be cherished and protected, to change course in order to follow where He leads, to testify of His kingship, to be cleansed of sin and made new, and to be established and carried along the way.

And being carried is right where this new Bible study picks up.

Pun not intended but also not deleted.

Just as season 2 of *The Chosen* depicts more of Jesus's way of living and being and teaching, so does the Sermon on the Mount. In every word spoken that day, we see the

For Bible Nerds (like us) Who Want to Know

Two of the four Gospels in the New Testament have summaries of the Sermon on the Mount: the Gospel of Matthew and the Gospel of Luke. Matthew has the longer summary (three chapters totaling 111 verses in Matthew 5–7), and Luke has the shorter summary (33 verses in Luke 6:17–49). While we will make the occasional reference to Luke's account (four "blessed" statements in Luke 6:20–23 and four corresponding "woe" statements in Luke 6:24–26), this study will primarily focus on Matthew's lengthier list of nine "blessed" statements.

Incidentally, is anyone surprised that Matthew's account of the sermon is the longer one?

Yeah, neither are we.

character, power, and promises of the One who carries us. Once we belong to Him, we're not only given a new identity, we're ushered into a new reality. One that is sure, imminent, and permanent. And so—

We have hope no matter our circumstances.

We have assurances and riches and resources no matter our circumstances.

We are blessed no matter our circumstances because God's favor is upon us.

That said, this new reality is not automatically seen or understood by spiritually untrained eyes. And wrapping our heads around God's favor—understanding it, accepting it in spite of who we know our sinful selves to be, prioritizing it over other things, and allowing it to fundamentally change the way we see and experience the world—brings with it some intrinsic hang-ups.

Hang-up 1: What We Care About

"If you then, who are evil, know how to give good gifts to your children, how much more will your Father who is in heaven give good things to those who ask him!"
Matthew 7:11

The key to experiencing all the "blessed" feels is to value God's favor more than we value earthly things. That doesn't mean earthly things don't matter or that they aren't gifts from Him. Of course God gives good gifts to His children, which include earthly things, and we should be thankful. We should steward our relationships, health, and finances well. But we should also hold them loosely, recognizing that God, His presence, and our future home with Him in heaven are the only things our hearts fundamentally need.

But holding our lives loosely is hard.

Hang-up 2: Works vs. Grace

Even after being saved by grace, most of us return to our default works-based setting, which means we tend to see the Beatitudes as things we must do in order to secure God's blessings. *I didn't earn God's forgiveness or the eternal life that freely came with it, but by golly, through good behavior and my own spiritual fortitude, I'm gonna earn more of His favor along the way.*

"For by grace you have been saved through faith. And this is not your own doing; it is the gift of God, not a result of works, so that no one may boast."
Ephesians 2:8–9

So ridiculous.

The truth is, when we believe Jesus is who He said He is and we surrender our lives to Him, **the blessings become ours because they're His**. By His grace, He offers His life to us along with everything it includes. The blessings are ours already.

But comprehending blessing so extraordinary and so freely given is really hard.

Hang-up 3: Blessed, Not Easy

The Beatitudes actually present us with a challenge, but it's not a challenge to work harder so we can earn more of God's blessings. Nor should we hear Jesus's sermon and respond by burning down our houses in order to become poor, or try to get non-Christians to beat us up in order to be persecuted.

Duh.

Instead, the challenge is to recognize God's favor in our lives *in spite of our difficult circumstances*, because having His favor doesn't mean our lives will be easy. Clearly God doesn't fix all our problems or Jesus wouldn't have said, "Blessed are those who mourn." Indeed, there is still disease and death, heartache and struggle, persecution and poverty. God doesn't always change our earthly circumstances, which is why Jesus took the time to illuminate the bigger picture: God is with us in every circumstance, *which changes every circumstance*. He

"I have said these things to you, that in me you may have peace. In the world you will have tribulation. But take heart; I have overcome the world."
John 16:33

long-suffers alongside us. He comforts us in the mess. He reminds us of our future with Him in heaven, where He promises there will be no more tears.

But seeing beyond our difficult circumstances is really, **really** hard.

The In-Between John 11:1–44

The story of Mary, Martha, and their brother Lazarus has massive significance, and not just because Jesus brought a dead man back to life. Lazarus had been gravely ill and his sisters sent word to Jesus—who decided *not* to return in time to heal His friend. By the time Jesus did go back, Lazarus had been dead four days. The community, along with Mary and Martha, was devastated and grieving, but Jesus told them to reopen the tomb and commanded Lazarus to come out.

And then he did.

> "Jesus lifted up his eyes and said, 'Father, I thank you that you have heard me. I knew that you always hear me, but I said this on account of the people standing around, that they may believe that you sent me.' When he had said these things, he cried out with a loud voice, 'Lazarus, come out.' The man who had died came out, his hands and feet bound with linen strips, and his face wrapped with a cloth. Jesus said to them, 'Unbind him, and let him go.'"
>
> John 11:41–44

Jesus said to him, "I am the way, and the truth, and the life. No one comes to the Father except through me." John 14:6

The obvious takeaway is that Jesus has power over life and death. He *is* life and gives life—physically, in the case of Lazarus, but also spiritually. When we surrender to Jesus, we're "born again"; our sins forgiven and forgotten, we're made new. But there's a second extraordinary aspect of this famous story, because before Jesus raised Lazarus from the dead, He wept.

"Now when Mary came to where Jesus was and saw him, she fell

at his feet, saying to him, 'Lord, if you had been here, my brother

would not have died.' When Jesus saw her weeping, and the Jews

who had come with her also weeping, he was deeply moved in

his spirit and greatly troubled. And he said, 'Where have you laid

him?' They said to him, 'Lord, come and see.' Jesus wept."

John 11:32–35

Jesus didn't weep for Lazarus. He knew His friend was about

to walk out of the tomb and that many would glorify God as a

result. The circumstances were, in fact, part of a divine master

plan to prove to the people watching that Jesus was, indeed, the

Messiah they'd been waiting for.

> Messiah:
> the promised deliverer
> of the Jewish nation (or
> "Savior") prophesied
> in the Hebrew Bible
> or Old Testament.

Which means Jesus wept because the people He loved were weeping.

Unlike Jesus, Mary and Martha didn't know their brother would be raised. They were *in between*, that part of the story where (1) they knew and loved Jesus but (2) their circumstances were still overwhelming. Not only had they lost a loved one; they'd lost their provider and protector. Women in ancient times wholly depended on the men in their lives (their fathers or husbands or, in the absence of both, their brothers) for the very roofs over their heads. Which meant these women were not only devastated by their loss; they were also afraid.

To add insult to their injured hearts, their Messiah, *who was also their friend*, didn't come to their rescue. At least, not in the way they had asked Him to, which may be why Mary didn't immediately go to Jesus when He arrived—she stayed inside. When she did speak to Him, she blamed Him. "Lord, if you had been here, my brother would not have died" (v. 32).

Jesus wasn't mad at Mary for being overwhelmed with grief and fear. And anger. He knew she was in the in-between, stuck in hard circumstances, the future unknown to her.

It was, in fact, her grief that made Him grieve—because He was in the in-between with her. That space between calling Jesus "Lord" for the first time and being delivered from the broken, brutal world we live in. That space where even though we've put our faith in Jesus, heartache, worry, and confusion still churn. That space where the way forward is sometimes unsure and circumstances can cause us to lose sight of what's true—which is exactly why Jesus took the time to teach us what's true, no matter how things appear.

> Blessed are the poor in spirit.
> Blessed are those who mourn.
> Blessed are the meek.
> Blessed are those who hunger and thirst for righteousness.
> Blessed are the merciful.
> Blessed are the pure in heart.
> Blessed are the peacemakers.
> Blessed are those who are persecuted for righteousness' sake.

In the Sermon on the Mount, Jesus describes our new reality—our actual reality, regardless of our circumstances. He describes things we can't always see but remain true anyway; a kingdom not visible to the unsaved or spiritually untrained eye, but when brought into focus, provides hope that supersedes the hard things. In His sermon, Jesus describes the truth about what matters: who we are when we belong to Him, what we have when we belong to Him, where we're going because we belong to Him, and what it means to be blessed in the in-between and unto eternity.

Which means congratulations are in order.

God's favor is upon you.

John, Son of Zebedee (a.k.a., the Beloved Disciple)

Recognized as "the disciple whom Jesus loved" (John 13:23; 19:26; 20:2; 21:7, 20), the apostle John, son of Zebedee, authored five New Testament books (the Gospel of John, the letters of 1–3 John, and Revelation), totaling about 21 percent of the New Testament. John was the only named apostle present at Jesus's crucifixion, at which time Jesus assigned the care of His mother, Mary, to him (John 19:25–27). Church tradition reports that John was a leader of the church in Ephesus in the middle of the first century. After his exile on the nearby island of Patmos, where he had the visions described in the book of Revelation, John returned to Ephesus. Likely to have been the youngest of Jesus's apostles, John is thought to be the only one to die of old age rather than as a martyr (sometime between AD 98–106).

James, Son of Zebedee (a.k.a., James the Greater)

Jesus dubbed James and his brother John the "Sons of Thunder" (Mark 3:17), perhaps for their harsh response to opposition (Mark 9:38; Luke 9:54). Or perhaps it was their father, Zebedee, who was the "thunderous" one. Or perhaps it was all of the above since apples tend to fall near the tree. Regardless, James was in the inner circle of Jesus's friends, which included Peter, James, and John. According to Acts 12:1–3, he was the first of the apostles to die as a martyr for the gospel, being put to death by the sword at the command of Herod Agrippa I (AD 41) before persecution dispersed the apostles from Jerusalem (Acts 8:1; 11:19).

THE POOR IN SPIRIT
and the sons of thunder

"Blessed are the poor in spirit, for theirs is the kingdom of heaven."

Matthew 5:3

SAMARITAN TRADER: You Jewish boys are far from home.

JESUS: Yes, as a matter of fact we are. Shalom to you too.

SAMARITAN TRADER: Here's our traditional Jewish greeting for you …

(The traders hurl rocks at Jesus but miss. John and Big James stand in shock but quickly process what they've seen. Before the brothers can spring forward, Jesus thrusts His arms to the side, stopping them like a gate.)

JESUS: Don't lift a finger.

SAMARITAN TRADER: That was a warning.

BIG JAMES: Try it again and see what happens!

JESUS: Quiet, Big James.

SAMARITAN TRADER: Shalom to you too.

(Members of the caravan spit on John as they pass by.)

JOHN: You filthy dogs!

JESUS: I said quiet!

(The brothers practically shake with rage. When the caravan has passed, John pivots so that his back is to the traders, his face close to Jesus's.)

JOHN *(practically hissing)*: Let us do something.

JESUS: And what would that achieve?

JOHN: Defending Your honor.

BIG JAMES: They reviled and humiliated You.

JOHN: They deserve to have bolts of lightning rain down and incinerate them.

BIG JAMES: Yes, fire from the heavens!

JESUS: Fire?

JOHN: You said we could do things like that. Say the word, and it will happen.

(Jesus stares at them.)

BIG JAMES: Why not? We knew we couldn't trust these people; we shouldn't have come here in the first place. They don't deserve You.

(John's eyes search those of his Master wildly.)

JESUS: Why do you think I had you work Melech's field? What was I trying to teach you?

BIG JAMES: To help?

JESUS: You think it was just to be more helpful, or to be better farmers? It was to show you that what we're doing here will last for generations. What I told Photina at the well, and what she then told so many others … it's sowing seeds that will have a lasting impact for lifetimes. Can you not see what's happening here? These people that you hate so much are believing in Me without even seeing miracles … it's the message, the truth that we're giving them. And you're going to get in the way of that because a few people from a region you don't like were mean to you? They're not worthy? What—you're so much better, you're more worthy?

JESUS (CONT'D): Well, let me tell you something: you're not! That's the whole point. It's why I'm here.

Trading Up

Right before his account of the SOM, Matthew commented on the arrest of John the Baptist and said, "From that time Jesus began to preach, saying, 'Repent, for **the kingdom of heaven is at hand**'" (Matt. 4:17). Which meant Jesus's followers were launching—however slowly and imperfectly this side of eternity—into His kingdom way of living. They were trading in their old way of seeing, thinking, and behaving for a new way, similar to the trade Jesus described in Matthew 11:28–29 when He said, "Come to me, all who labor and are heavy laden, and I will give you rest. Take my yoke upon you, and learn from me, for I am gentle and lowly in heart, and you will find rest for your souls."

SOM = Sermon on the Mount ... because we're already weary of typing it out.

Indeed, the world has a way of burdening us, sometimes beyond what we can bear. Jesus acknowledged our pain and struggle by inviting us to bring it all to Him: to trade our burdens for His rest, our neediness and weakness for His tender care and limitless strength, our chaos and confusion for His peace, our brokenness for His wholeness.

He invites us to trade in. To trade up.

Same thing is true in the SOM. Jesus took the time to describe the blessings we receive when we give our lives to Him—and it isn't just heaven. It's life to the fullest here and now because we belong to Him and **He is with us**, carrying us and comforting us, equipping us and satisfying us, providing for and promising us a kingdom in which we're heirs of creation itself! The life our Creator and King offers and freely gives to those who follow Him is far better than what the world offers or could ever give—if only we'd see and embrace our new reality as sons and daughters of the Most High.

"[Jesus] appointed the twelve: Simon (to whom he gave the name Peter); James the son of Zebedee and John the brother of James (to whom he gave the name Boanerges, that is, Sons of Thunder)."
Mark 3:16–17

But more often than not, we think and behave like the Sons of Thunder.

Your Turn

1. What burdens are you attempting to carry in your own wisdom or strength?

You've Got to Be Kidding

Samaritan:
a person from Samaria.

"And [Jesus] sent messengers ahead of him, who went and entered a village of the Samaritans, to make preparations for him. But the people did not receive him, because his face was set toward Jerusalem. And when his disciples James and John saw it, they said, 'Lord, do you want us to tell fire to come down from heaven and consume them?'"

Luke 9:52–54

Jews in Jesus's day looked down on Samaritans as the tainted descendants of Israelites who had intermarried with pagan foreigners (Luke 9:51–56; 10:25–37; 17:11–19). Thus, the Samaritans developed their own religious worship center at Mount Gerizim, their own version of the Old Testament Scriptures, and their own particular beliefs.

Insert sarcastic tone here, because the stupidity and ugliness of racism is nothing new.

James and John spent a lot of time with Jesus. They personally experienced His forgiveness, patience, and graciousness. They watched Him welcome all kinds of people with all kinds of problems—*even* Samaritans—with no strings attached. They witnessed Him heal the spiritually possessed and the physically oppressed. They saw Him turn the other cheek when He was mocked or rejected, pouring Himself out to serve and to seek and to save. Yet somehow, after all that, the brothers thought Jesus might give a thumbs-up to their murder plan.

Oh the irony of the Thunder Twins calling for harsh punishment of others when they'd been on the receiving end of unmerited grace. But that's what we humans tend to do. We recognize our own desperate need for Jesus, only to forget it once we know Him. We compare ourselves to those we deem worse, judging the hearts and minds of others as though we're in any position to do so, all the while failing to extend the very love and mercy we've been repeatedly shown by God Himself.

James and John were not actually twins, but it sounds sort of funny to say it that way.

But blessed are the poor in spirit.

Being poor in spirit isn't a money thing—though being financially poor sometimes makes it easier to be poor in spirit. *Lack* of any kind has a way of tenderizing our hearts and exposing our real need. Conversely, wealth sometimes makes it harder to be poor in spirit since it fosters self-sufficiency and even pride, which are enemies of the lowly posture required to be "poor in spirit." Indeed, some of the terms for "poor" in the Bible were regularly used for those so lowly, so disadvantaged and distressed, they needed outside intervention— which isn't far from how we sometimes use the word today. For example, when we see a news report of a horrific accident and a man being cut from his car and rushed to the hospital, we might say, "That poor guy." Of course, we're not referring to his bank account. We're referring to his desperate need for intervention and help.

Grace: good stuff God gives that we don't deserve to get.

"Woe to you who are rich, for you have received your consolation." Luke 6:24

In the Sermon on the Mount, the "poor" Jesus refers to are those who are ready and willing to look to God for help. Because when we recognize our own spiritual bankruptcy—our desperate need to be saved from sin and all its consequences—we get real low real fast. And if we're smart, we stay there. To be poor in spirit means to take a knee, now and forevermore. It means to live in surrender to our Savior, relying on Him for the help we can't possibly provide ourselves.

Lowliness: humble in manner or spirit; free from pride.

To be sure, the Samaritans who offended James and John had their own sin issues, and their prejudice toward the Jews closed their ears and hearts to who Jesus really was.

But then their rejection of Jesus led to the disciples' rejection of Jesus's authority—at least in that moment. Because calling down fire from heaven to destroy an entire village is the *opposite* of what Jesus was teaching His followers to do. They took their eyes off their leader and hardcore stared at their circumstances, which caused their self-righteous self-sufficiency to wield its ugly head.

Alternatively, when we're bent low, it's Jesus who lifts our heads. And it's Jesus who leads us on. Which means those who are poor in spirit don't have the time or inclination to judge others because they're too busy (1) doing battle with their own ongoing sin, (2) continually experiencing the grace that saved them in the first place, and (3) keeping their eyes on Jesus and His kingdom.

A kingdom that, incidentally, is already here.

Your Turn

2. In what ways are you like the Sons of Thunder?

3. What lack are you experiencing in your life, and what deeper need is it working to expose?

4. Read Isaiah 66:1–2 and underline what God says about those who are poor in spirit.

"Thus says the LORD:
'Heaven is my throne,
and the earth is my footstool;
what is the house that you would build for me,
and what is the place of my rest?
All these things my hand has made,
and so all these things came to be,
declares the LORD.
But this is the one to whom I will look:
he who is humble and contrite in spirit
and trembles at my word.'"

Contrite: feeling or expressing remorse or penitence.

The Wheat and the Weeds

"He put another parable before them, saying, 'The kingdom of heaven may be compared to a man who sowed good seed in his field, but while his men were sleeping, his enemy came and sowed weeds among the wheat and went away. So when the plants came up and bore grain, then the weeds appeared also. And the servants of the master of the house came and said to him, "Master, did you not sow good seed in your field? How then does it have weeds?" He said to them, "An enemy has done this." So the servants said to him, "Then do you want us to go and gather them?" But he said, "No, lest in gathering the weeds you root up the wheat along with them. Let both grow together until the harvest, and at harvest time I will tell the reapers, 'Gather the weeds first and bind them in bundles to be burned, but gather the wheat into my barn.'"

Matthew 13:24–30

For Bible Nerds (like us) Who Want to Know

The first Beatitude (Matt. 5:3) and the last Beatitude (Matt. 5:10) both close with "theirs is the kingdom of heaven," which means that must be a significant promise for the blessed. But what exactly does it mean?

Well, for the first-century Jews hearing the SOM, the "kingdom of heaven" (a.k.a., "kingdom of God") didn't merely mean going to heaven when you die. To be included in a kingdom of some kind was to be ruled by a king and to enjoy the benefits (or hardships) of that king.

Those listening to Jesus's sermon were suffering under Roman rule with Caesar as king, and they were longing to be rescued from his unjust rule. And the "kingdom of heaven" was their long-hoped-for, God-established society wherein the Messiah would be King, ruling with love and justice over His chosen people in a land of peace and fulfillment.

Of note is that this particular blessing is spelled out, *not* in the future tense, but in the present tense: "theirs IS the kingdom of heaven." Not WILL BE. Which means the Jews might've been incorrect in some of their assumptions about the details, but they weren't wrong to believe the kingdom is already here.

Strange that Jesus's parable about the man who planted good seeds in a field, and his enemy who planted bad seeds in the same field, somehow describes the kingdom of heaven. But also, it totally does. Because we're living in the age of planting and gathering—the part of the story where God is calling His people from every tribe, nation, and tongue in order to build His heavenly kingdom. Those who bend their knee to the King belong to that kingdom, and it belongs to them. They are the good seeds that sprout and spread in the midst of, *and in spite of,* a weed-filled, dying world.

Jesus taught His disciples about a new way to live—a heavenly kingdom way that begins on earth. He *wasn't* merely teaching about making good choices, though we should obey God's Word and try to be more like Jesus, and we should definitely NOT pray for fire to rain down on people's heads. But while our choices are important, they're *not* the focus of the Beatitudes in the SOM. Rather, Jesus wanted His followers to see and understand their **new reality** and that life here isn't all there is. Jesus came offering Himself and everything that belongs to Him, which includes His kingdom membership. When we embrace Him, we're in, despite the fact that we still live here.

And the knowledge of that should change everything. We're here, but only for now. Our circumstances are difficult, but only for now. Our pain and

"For this light momentary affliction is preparing for us an eternal weight of glory beyond all comparison, as we look not to the things that are seen but to the things that are unseen. For the things that are seen are transient, but the things that are unseen are eternal."
2 Corinthians 4:17–18

suffering are real, but only for now. Sin and sickness and strife are part of our lives, but only for now.

Also part of our lives right now?

Access to the King.
We can actually approach the
God of the universe.

"Blessed be the God and Father of our Lord Jesus Christ, who
has blessed us in Christ with every spiritual blessing in the
heavenly places, even as he chose us in him before the foundation
of the world, that we should be holy and blameless before him.
In love he predestined us for adoption to himself
as sons [and daughters] through Jesus Christ, according
to the purpose of his will, to the praise of his glorious
grace, with which he has blessed us in the Beloved."
Ephesians 1:3–6

"Therefore, brothers, since **we have confidence
to enter the holy places** by the blood of
Jesus, by the new and living way that he opened for
us through the curtain, that is, through his flesh, and
since we have a great priest over the house of God,
let us draw near with a true heart in full assurance
of faith, with our hearts sprinkled clean from an evil
conscience and our bodies washed with pure water."
Hebrews 10:19–22

The high priest had to pass through a curtain to reach the Holy of Holies in the temple—the place where God's presence dwelled. When Christ died on the cross, the curtain was torn in two, opening up and offering the presence of God to us all.

Access to the King's power.
We are not left powerless
in the world today.

"For the kingdom of God does not consist in talk but in power."
1 Corinthians 4:20

"For God gave us a spirit not of fear but of
power and love and self-control."
2 Timothy 1:7

"His divine power has granted to us all things
that pertain to life and godliness, through the knowledge of
him who called us to his own glory and excellence."
2 Peter 1:3

The attention of the King.
Our needs are brought before the
Father by Jesus Himself.

"Who is to condemn? Christ Jesus is the one who died—more than that, who was raised—who is at the right hand of God, who indeed is interceding for us. Who shall separate us from the love of Christ? Shall tribulation, or distress, or persecution, or famine, or nakedness, or danger, or sword?… No, in all these things we are more than conquerors through him who loved us. For I am sure that neither death nor life, nor angels nor rulers, nor things present nor things to come, nor powers, nor height nor depth, nor anything else in all creation, will be able to separate us from the love of God in Christ Jesus our Lord."

Romans 8:34–39

"Consequently, [Jesus] is able to save to the uttermost those
who draw near to God through him, since he always
lives to make intercession for them."

Hebrews 7:25

The presence of the King.
God is with us all the time.
In all the things.

"And I will ask the Father, and he will give you another Helper,
to be with you forever, even the Spirit of truth, whom the world
cannot receive, because it neither sees him nor knows him. You know
him, for he dwells with you and will be in you."

John 14:16–17

"But the Helper, the Holy Spirit, whom the
Father will send in my name, he will teach you all things
and bring to your remembrance all that I have said to you."

John 14:26

"Therefore, since we have been justified by faith, we have peace with God through our Lord Jesus Christ. Through him we have also obtained access by faith into this grace in which we stand, and we rejoice in hope of the glory of God. Not only that, but we rejoice in our sufferings, knowing that suffering produces endurance, and endurance produces character, and character produces hope, and hope does not put us to shame, because **God's love has been poured into our hearts through the Holy Spirit who has been given to us.**"

Romans 5:1–5

Your Turn

5. In light of the preceding verses, describe God's favor toward the poor in spirit.

6. In His parable of the weeds, Jesus illustrated the coexistence of His kingdom and the broken world we live in. How are you experiencing this tension in your life?

God's favor   Good choices

Praise, devotion,   God's favor
peace, joy

7. Good choices are good and they flow from our love and devotion to Jesus. But our choices don't determine our daily dose of God's favor—that's ours in full already because Jesus has secured it, which means we can't earn favor before *or after* we belong to the kingdom. How should knowing that impact any "Sons of Thunder" tendencies you may have?

8. Read Revelation 21:1–4 and describe the fullness of the kingdom that lies ahead.

MELECH'S FARM (NIGHT)

(Night has fallen and Jesus and His disciples are seated around their new friend's fire, finishing their meal. Melech's wife, Chedva, and daughter, Rebecca, sit at his side.)

SIMON *(laughing)*: The boat almost flipped … then the net strained so hard I thought my arms would come out of their sockets.

ANDREW: And James and John took their sweet time coming to help us.

(Andrew turns to John and Big James with a chuckle. The brothers, withdrawn and bothered, don't return the gesture.)

SIMON: I had to call for help five times before you moved.

MELECH: And so you followed Him. All the way into Samaria.

MATTHEW: We did suggest the alternate route along the Jordan.

MELECH: You didn't think it could be … dangerous? For You?

(Chedva shoots Melech a forbidding look. Jesus stares into Melech's eyes.)

JESUS: Of course.

(Chedva clears her throat.)

CHEDVA: When I was a little girl, my father told me the Messiah would bring an end to pain and suffering. If You are who people are saying You are, when will You do that?

(The faces of the disciples glow in the firelight. They're interested in the answer too.)

JESUS: I am here to preach the good news of the kingdom of heaven, a kingdom that is not of this world, a kingdom that is coming soon, where, yes, sorrow and sighing will flee away. I make a way for people to access that kingdom. But in this world, bones will still break, hearts will still break, but in the end, the light will overcome darkness.

Prayer Focus

Talk to God about your spiritual poverty and inability to earn His favor. Thank Him for pursuing you, and for choosing you to follow Jesus and enjoy His kingdom. Ask Him to empower you by the Holy Spirit to live according to His kingdom values even when your circumstances are difficult.

Sample Prayer

Dear Lord,

Thank You for extending Your generous and undeserved love toward me. Forgive me for all the ways I attempt to earn the favor You've freely offered in Jesus, rather than simply acknowledging my spiritual poverty and dependence on You. Help me to acknowledge it, Lord.

Thank You for extending to me Your kingdom. Through Your Holy Spirit, help me to allow Your kingdom to break through in my life, even today. Despite my current circumstances, help me recognize my happiness in You and all the gifts You have already provided.

Amen.

Nathanael (a.k.a., Bartholomew)

While at first reluctant, Nathanael became a follower of Jesus as a result of Philip's persistent encouragement to investigate the possibility that Jesus might be the promised Messiah (John 1:43–51). John explicitly named Nathanael among the apostles (John 21:2), though the name Nathanael does not otherwise appear in the four Gospels; rather, they name "Bartholomew" in their lists of apostles (Matt. 10:1–4; Mark 3:13–19; Luke 6:12–16; Acts 1:13), and we're led to conclude that the one man had two names: Nathanael Bartholomew. Incidentally, double-naming was common in the first century, even among the twelve apostles (for example, Simon Peter and Levi Matthew). Various traditions say that Nathanael Bartholomew later ministered in Turkey with Philip (not a surprise), in Parthia with Andrew (the region of modern-day Iran and Afghanistan), in Egypt with Peter, and even as far as India. A variety of traditions report quite different means for Nathanael's martyrdom: flayed alive, crucified, beaten to death, beheaded, and/or drowned in the sea (believed to have occurred in AD 82).

Philip

The Gospel of John reports that two of John the Baptist's disciples became early followers of Jesus and explicitly names Andrew, who then recruited his brother Simon Peter (John 1:35–42). Like Peter and Andrew, Philip was from Bethsaida, and he is known for recruiting Nathanael (a.k.a., Bartholomew) to follow Jesus as well (John 1:43–51). Thus, Philip is sometimes presumed to be the second of John the Baptist's former disciples to follow Jesus. Philip is mentioned by name several times in the Gospel of John (John 6:5–7; 12:20–22; 14:6–10) and is said to have ministered later in Turkey, Tunisia, and northern Africa. He was martyred by stoning (AD 54).

Lesson 2

THOSE WHO MOURN
and the God who sees

"Blessed are those who mourn, for they shall be comforted."

Matthew 5:4

CAESAREA (DAY)

(Nathanael walks into a bar in Caesarea, defeated. He all but collapses onto his stool and addresses the bartender.)

NATHANAEL: Your strongest. And cheapest.

BARTENDER: Is something wrong, friend?

NATHANAEL: Yes.

BARTENDER: Did someone die?

NATHANAEL: Yes.

BARTENDER: I'm sorry for your loss. Was it sudden?

NATHANAEL: I think … it was a long time coming for him, but it felt sudden.

BARTENDER *(furrows brow)*: Hmm. Tell me about him.

NATHANAEL: He was an architect. It was what he wanted to be his whole life.

BARTENDER: Sad.

NATHANAEL: He came from nothing. Worked his way up. Loved God. He wanted to build synagogues eventually. I know that's not very popular around here … one with colonnades that sing. Parapets that practically pray. Vaunted halls that draw the soul upward to God. That's what God made him for. Or so he thought.

BARTENDER (*shaking his head*): He sounds like an ambitious guy. What did he die of?

NATHANAEL: Hubris.

(*Bartender gives him a long look.*)

NATHANAEL (CONT'D): It's me, by the way. I'm the dead man in the story.

BARTENDER: Yeah, yeah I got that.

NATHANAEL: I just wanted to be clear.

(*LATER THAT DAY, OUTSIDE OF CAESAREA*)

(*Nathanael drags his feet through a rural area. He sits under a fig tree, filled with remorse. He looks around; there's no one for miles. He's alone. He pulls architectural drawings out of his satchel and rifles through them.*)

NATHANAEL:

This was done for You.

(*He glances at the sky.*)

Blessed are You … blessed are You, Lord our God, King of the Universe …

(*He sighs, shakes his head, as though he's trying to say whatever he can come up with.*)

Hear, Israel, the Lord is our God, the Lord is One.

(*He strikes a flint against a rock and sets fire to the drawings. As they start to burn …*)

Hear my prayer, O Lord; let my cry come to You … do not hide Your face from me in the day of my distress …

(*Tears flow.*)

Incline Your ear to me; answer me speedily in the day when I call …

(*He looks up again, pauses.*)

No? This was done for You! Do not hide Your face from me! Do You see me?

(He sits back under the tree, hugging his knees to his chin while he watches his dreams burn.)

NATHANAEL (CONT'D): Do You see me?

Hope Deferred

Let's be honest … happiness is a better selling point than "comfort in grief." In fact, our human tendency is to assume that following Jesus = more happiness. We may not always be aware that's our spiritual expectation, but when life goes awry and grief sets in, we quickly rear back at God with questions like:

How could You? Why would You? Don't You see me? Don't You love me?

The truth is that grief can be utterly derailing. We know God has the power to heal, but He doesn't always heal. At least not always on this side of eternity. We know He has the power to save our reputations, our jobs, our loved ones, our hopes, our dreams—but sometimes He doesn't. We know God has the power to change and fix and protect and provide in exactly the ways we want Him to, so when He doesn't, it calls into question His love for us and even His very character.

But "blessed are those who mourn."

In the face of suffering or death, God's comfort in grief seems like a pretty pathetic consolation prize. Except to those who've received it.

Your Turn

1. In what ways have you experienced grief in your life? What has your response been to it?

The Good and the Grief

"The next day Jesus decided to go to Galilee. He found Philip and
said to him, 'Follow me.' Now Philip was from Bethsaida, the city of
Andrew and Peter. Philip found Nathanael and said to him, 'We have
found him of whom Moses in the Law and also the prophets wrote,
Jesus of Nazareth, the son of Joseph.' Nathanael said to him, 'Can
anything good come out of Nazareth?' Philip said to him, 'Come
and see.' Jesus saw Nathanael coming toward him and said of him,
'Behold, an Israelite indeed, in whom there is no deceit!' Nathanael
said to him, 'How do you know me?' Jesus answered him, 'Before
Philip called you, when you were under the fig tree, I saw you.'"

John 1:43–48

We can't skip grief. If we could, we wouldn't be capable of fully experiencing love or laughter or peace or any of the other good things, because grief reflects our capacity for the good things. At its core, grief is the soul's recognition that the world isn't what God created it to be. That loss, brokenness, and death are, in fact, the antithesis of the what He made. And, like us, He grieves—but not just because our sinfulness destroyed His beautiful world. He grieves with us because He loves us and because nothing we experience escapes His purview.

"For we know that the whole creation has been groaning together in the pains of childbirth until now. And not only the creation, but we ourselves, who have the firstfruits of the Spirit, groan inwardly as we wait eagerly for adoption as sons, the redemption of our bodies."
Romans 8:22–23

Which brings us to Nathanael. It's probably safe to surmise that the soon-to-be-disciple didn't follow Jesus based solely on His ability to know people's whereabouts. No doubt the fig tree thing was cool, but it wasn't the only thing Jesus knew, because in their brief exchange, Jesus revealed a much more intimate knowledge: "Behold, an Israelite indeed, in whom there is no deceit!"

"Can anything good come out of Nazareth?"

Based on Nathanael's comment to Philip about Jesus's hometown, we can deduce he didn't hide much. He "spoke his truth." He was in the habit of "telling it like it is." Or more accurately, he was opinionated, perhaps prideful, a little rude, and kinda prejudiced. And Jesus clearly knew it, gracious as He was in the way He characterized it. He'd seen Nathanael under the fig tree and all the days before. He knew Nathanael's life story, his hurts and his triumphs, his fears and his dreams, his weaknesses and his strengths. Jesus knew what made Nathanael tick. Knew his very thoughts, whether under that fig tree or standing in front of the Creator Himself.   *"Behold, an Israelite in whom there is no deceit!"*

Such knowledge—such comfort to be so intimately known—converted the flawed-but-still-called Israelite in an instant; his grief and heartache forevermore to be carried by the One who saw him. The same One who sees us when we're alone, when we're grieving, and before we're even aware He's there.

Your Turn

2. In episode 2, Nathanael is grieving under the fig tree. While we don't actually know what he was thinking about in that moment, according to Psalm 34:18, what *do* we know?

3. According to Exodus 3:7, what *do* we know?

4. According to 2 Corinthians 1:3–4, what *do* we know?

Out of Ashes

"The Spirit of the Lord GOD is upon me, because the LORD has anointed me to bring good news to the poor; he has sent me to bind up the brokenhearted, to proclaim liberty to the captives, and the opening of the prison to those who are bound; **to proclaim the year of the LORD's favor,** and the day of vengeance of our God; to comfort all who mourn; to grant to those who mourn in Zion— to give them a beautiful headdress instead of ashes, the oil of gladness instead of mourning, the garment of praise instead of a faint spirit; that they may be called oaks of righteousness, the planting of the LORD, that he may be glorified."

Isaiah 61:1–3

Putting ashes on one's head was an expression of sorrow, and conversely, putting oil in one's hair was an expression of rejoicing.

"As it is, I rejoice, not because you were grieved, but because you were grieved into repenting. For you felt a godly grief, so that you suffered no loss through us. For godly grief produces a repentance that leads to salvation without regret, whereas worldly grief produces death."
2 Corinthians 7:9–10

Through the Old Testament prophet Isaiah, God promised that the Spirit-anointed Messiah would turn sorrow into rejoicing. But what does that even mean, since we've already established that He doesn't always remove the cause(s) of our sorrow?

There are simply so many reasons to grieve. Sometimes poverty or persecution can lead us to grief. Sickness and death do for sure, not to mention coming face to face with our own sinfulness. And God actually *uses* our grief and our distress and our abject need to draw us to Himself. The comfort expressed in the context of Isaiah 61 was for those who looked to Him for forgiveness of their sins (Isa. 59:9–15) and for help in the hardship they were experiencing (Isa. 60:14–18). As a result of their grief, they looked to Him because of what He could do for them that they couldn't do for themselves.

We, in fact, cannot comfort ourselves. Not truly, not profoundly. We can look on the bright side of life, we can count our blessings and measure cups half-full, but in the deep recesses of our hearts, we can't be to ourselves what we desperately need. And neither can anything or anyone else in the whole wide world. We can sometimes temporarily affect our own happiness, but we can't be the balm we need when happiness flees. And … it … flees.

As we saw in the story about Mary, Martha, and their brother Lazarus, Jesus grieves too. In fact, in Isaiah 53, He's referred to as "a man of sorrows and acquainted with grief, and as one from whom men hide their faces he was despised, and we esteemed him not" (v. 3).

"When Jesus saw [Mary] weeping, and the Jews who had come with her also weeping, he was deeply moved in his spirit and greatly troubled. And he said, 'Where have you laid him?' They said to him, 'Lord, come and see.' Jesus wept."
John 11:33–35

It's not often we think of Jesus as a man of sorrow. In fact, when life goes into the proverbial ditch, we tend to feel like God has done something *to us*, which means we miss entirely that He's grieving *with us*. While it's true that He's sovereign and sometimes allows hard things, it's also true that He remains present in the hard things—and that He's been *through* the hard things. Jesus lost people He loved to sickness and

Sovereign: having supreme or ultimate power (i.e., God knows and understands the things we don't know or see or understand yet).

death too, including His cousin John the Baptist (Matt. 14:1–12) and His earthly father (note the absence of Joseph in John 19:26–27). He lost His reputation in His hometown of Nazareth, probably along with a lot of His childhood friends (Luke 4:16–29). His entire life, He was plain and overlooked (Isa. 53:2). He was poor, so He experienced the physical discomfort of hunger pains and sleeping on the ground (Luke 2:6–7; 2 Cor. 8:9;

Heb. 4:14–15). He was rejected, betrayed, cast aside, misunderstood, mistreated, and ultimately murdered by the very people He came to save (John 19:1–30).

He was indeed a man of sorrows, intimately acquainted with grief.

Including yours.

God sees you. He knows what grieves you, and He is grieving with you. He grieves your grief, the loss of creation as He intended it to be, and the unending ripple effects of a world that's been broken and twisted and darkened. And He's offering Himself to you in the midst of your heartache. Think about that … the Creator of the universe, the all-powerful King, the Redeemer and Re-Creator—He sees *you*. And He sees what pains you.

He's not asking you to move on from your pain more quickly. He's not impatient with you or disappointed in your inability to be okay. He knows that with some forms of pain come scars of the past and/or fear of the future, and He's not responding to your confusion, anger, or uncertainty by pulling away from you. Like any good parent would respond to a hurting child, God moves toward you in your pain, which means blessed are you who mourn, because you will be comforted by the God who loves you, **the One who's favor is upon you**.

And the knowledge of that should change everything. We grieve, but God grieves with us; we are never alone. God sees us, intimately understands us, and moves toward us, never abandoning us to our pain—on the contrary. He holds us with a steadfast love and promises to turn our sadness into praise.

How?

By bending low to rescue us and heal us, the first day and all the days.

"But you, O LORD, are a shield about me,
my glory, and **the lifter of my head**."

Psalm 3:3

"The LORD is near to the brokenhearted
and saves the crushed in spirit."

Psalm 34:18

"The LORD your **God is in your midst**, a mighty one
who will save; he will rejoice over you with gladness; he will
quiet you by his love; he will exult over you with loud singing."

Zephaniah 3:17

"And we know that for those who love God
all things work together for good, for
those who are called according to his purpose."

Romans 8:28

**By dwelling with us, the Comforter Himself living
in our hearts and interceding on our behalf.**

"I will ask the Father, and he will give you another Helper, to be
with you forever, even the Spirit of truth, whom the world cannot
receive, because it neither sees him nor knows him. You know
him, **for he dwells with you and will be in you.**
I will not leave you as orphans; I will come to you."

John 14:16–18

"Likewise the Spirit helps us in our weakness. For we do not know what to pray for as we ought, **but the Spirit himself intercedes for us with groanings too deep for words.**"

Romans 8:26

By using us to comfort others and point them to the One who comforts us.

"Blessed be the God and Father of our Lord Jesus Christ, the Father of mercies and God of all comfort, who comforts us in all our affliction, **so that we may be able to comfort those who are in any affliction, with the comfort with which we ourselves are comforted** by God. For as we share abundantly in Christ's sufferings, so through Christ we share abundantly in comfort too. If we are afflicted, it is for your comfort and salvation; and if we are comforted, it is for your comfort, which you experience when you patiently endure the same sufferings that we suffer. Our hope for you is unshaken, for we know that as you share in our sufferings, you will also share in our comfort."

2 Corinthians 1:3–7

"Rejoice with those who rejoice, **weep with those who weep.**"

Romans 12:15

"For to me **to live is Christ, and to die is gain**.
If I am to live in the flesh, that means fruitful labor for
me. Yet which I shall choose I cannot tell. I am hard
pressed between the two. My desire is to depart and
be with Christ, for that is far better. But to remain
in the flesh is more necessary on your account."

Philippians 1:21–24

Paul was a disciple of Christ
who was persecuted for his
faith. He longed for death
because it meant being with
Jesus in heaven and the end
of his pain. But he also knew
that continuing in the flesh
meant telling more people
about Jesus and the comfort
and hope He provides.

**By giving our grief an expiration
date … because someday heaven.**

"Blessed are you who weep now, for **you shall laugh**."

Luke 6:21

"He will wipe away every tear from their eyes, and death shall be
no more, neither shall there be mourning, nor crying, nor pain
anymore, for **the former things have passed away**."

Revelation 21:4

"They shall hunger no more, neither thirst anymore; the
sun shall not strike them, nor any scorching heat. For the
Lamb in the midst of the throne will be their shepherd,
and he will guide them to springs of living water, and
God will wipe away every tear from their eyes."

Revelation 7:16–17

Your Turn

5. In light of the preceding verses, describe God's favor toward those who grieve.

6. Jesus read Isaiah 61 out loud in the synagogue of His hometown and then said, "Today this Scripture has been fulfilled in your hearing" (Luke 4:21)—i.e., *I'm the One Isaiah was talking about; the One who binds up the brokenhearted, frees the captives, and comforts those who mourn.*

How have you experienced Jesus in these ways throughout your life?

7. How does knowing that Jesus experienced grief throughout His entire earthly life impact the way you see your own?

8. Read John 10:14–15. Jesus is our Shepherd and He leads us to "springs of living water" (Rev. 7:17). But sometimes we get stuck in our grief and we resist His leading. How does knowing He's the good Shepherd—our Comforter, Empathizer, Rescuer, and Healer—make it easier to let Him lead you?

EXT. HOSTEL (NIGHT)

(Jesus steps out into the night and latches the door behind Him.)

PHILIP: Rabbi.

(Jesus turns to see Philip walking up with Nathanael. He adjusts his posture and seems genuinely honored.)

JESUS: Well, this is a good night.

(The two men are confused. To Philip—)

JESUS (CONT'D): Do you know who stands beside you?

PHILIP *(mystified)*: This is my friend, Nathanael.

(Jesus doesn't take His eyes off Nathanael.)

JESUS: Yes, the truth-teller.

(That gets their attention.)

NATHANAEL: I'm sorry?

JESUS: Man is often deceitful … and Israel began with Jacob, a bit of a deceiver, yes?

NATHANAEL: Yes?

JESUS: But one of the great things about you … you are a true Israelite, in whom there is no deceit.

NATHANAEL *(looking at Philip)*: What did you say about me?

(Philip shakes his head.)

NATHANAEL (CONT'D): What is this? How do You know me?

JESUS: I've known you long before Philip called you to come and see.

(Off Nathanael's sideways glance …)

JESUS (CONT'D):

Don't look at him; look at Me.

When you were in your lowest moment, and you were alone … I did not turn My face from you. I saw you. Under the fig tree.

(Nathanael's eyes widen.)

NATHANAEL: Rabbi.

(Philip is clueless but watches with excitement. Nathanael's eyes fill.)

JESUS: There it is.

NATHANAEL: You are the Son of God. The King of Israel.

PHILIP: I knew it!

JESUS: Well, that didn't take long.

PHILIP: He doesn't mess around.

JESUS: Because I said to you, "I saw you under the fig tree," you believe? You're going to see many greater things than that.

(Jesus grabs his shoulders, leans into Nathanael's now awestruck face.)

JESUS (CONT'D): Like Jacob, you're going to see heaven open, and the angels of God ascending and descending upon the Son of Man. That's Me, by the way.

NATHANAEL *(chuckles)*: Yeah, I got that.

JESUS: Good. I know you like to be clear.

(Andrew and Simon emerge from the hostel with urgency.)

ANDREW: Rabbi, sorry to interrupt, but John just arrived with a message from Syria.

JESUS: He came back?

SIMON: Yes, he said people are already gathering to meet You, many with afflictions to be healed. *(excited)* Your fame is spreading … the good kind.

ANDREW: You should rest, Rabbi. We should leave early.

JESUS: Thank you, boys.

(They hustle back in. Jesus turns back to Nathanael.)

JESUS (CONT'D):

So, you wanted to help build something that would cause prayer, and songs, something to bring souls closer to God, yes?

(Nathanael nods.)

Can you start tomorrow?

Prayer Focus

Talk to God about the things that are grieving you most right now. Thank Him for His full awareness of your situation and for the fact that He cares. Thank Him that He knows what mourning is like from personal experience and that He desires to share in your grief—to come alongside you and comfort you. Ask Him to empower you by His Holy Spirit to live joyfully—somehow—in the midst of your grief, and to look forward in hope to the time when all tears will be permanently wiped away.

Sample Prayer

Dear Lord,

You know more fully than even I do that there are things troubling me and causing me great sorrow. Thank You that You understand my grief.

Jesus, I recognize that in Your life on earth, You experienced all kinds of grief too, and it gives me some comfort to know that You truly understand and empathize with me.

Help me to be sad about the same things that make You sad. But at the same time, I need Your help to move forward in my life in the midst of this mourning. Through Your Holy Spirit, help me to allow joy in You to be a part of my life, even now while I wait.

Amen.

James, Son of Alphaeus (a.k.a., James the Lesser)

As the second of the two apostles named James, "James the son of Alphaeus" is consistently named as such in the lists of apostles (Matt. 10:3; Mark 3:18; Luke 6:15; Acts 1:13), but otherwise he's seldom mentioned in the New Testament. This James is sometimes confused *not* with the son of Zebedee but with Jesus's half brother James (who became an influential church leader in Acts and is more fully identified as "James the Just" in extrabiblical tradition—so many Jameses!).

Tradition suggests that Little James (as we refer to him in *The Chosen*) had a ministry with Armenian people and was martyred among them in Parthia, the region of modern-day Iran. His bones are said to have been relocated to the Cathedral of Saint James in the Armenian quarter of the Old City of Jerusalem. A later tradition suggests the possibility of Egypt as his place of ministry and martyrdom. The Church of the Holy Apostles in Rome is believed to have his remains alongside those of Philip—both being transferred there from Constantinople in the sixth century. He is said to have been clubbed to death and/or sawn in two (AD 70).

Lesson 3

THE MEEK
and the motherload

"Blessed are the meek, for they shall inherit the earth."

Matthew 5:5

EXT. SYRIAN CAMPSITE (AFTERNOON)

THADDAEUS: How's the line?

PHILIP: It's getting longer. I'll come back out soon and help you; I won't take my full break.

BIG JAMES: Where's Nathanael? It's my turn to replace him.

PHILIP: He said he's staying through; he doesn't want to stop his shift.

LITTLE JAMES *(indicating the game)*: Philip, take my place, see if you can make some headway; he's scary good.

(Thaddaeus and Little James leave, Philip heads toward Thomas. Matthew reads from his notes.)

MATTHEW: There have been over sixty people already, with fifty waiting in line currently, not including lepers and others who are still in line.

BIG JAMES: Did you say over fifty in the line now?

MATTHEW: Yes.

BIG JAMES: How long is this going to last?

MATTHEW: Well, it depends on each encounter, you have—

BIG JAMES: Never mind, I get it.

(Matthew pauses, then approaches Mary and Ramah, who have just emerged from their tents.)

RAMAH: Matthew, did you get some ideas from Philip?

MATTHEW: Yes, from the songs of David, a passage to study before we learn more.

BIG JAMES *(looking at his palm as he and John walk toward the fire)*: Bah, it's still bleeding.

JOHN: What … is that from the firewood from before?

BIG JAMES: Yes, and then when I pushed back the man who was rushing in the line, I cut it more on his bag. Hand me that rag.

(John grabs a cloth from the ground, and James wraps his hand.)

PHILIP: That same man you speak of bumped into me on his way out after Jesus healed his wife. I believe he's one of the men who arrived here last night.

BIG JAMES: Almost a four-hour walk this morning and we didn't even have a moment to settle in. I mean, it's great what He's doing, obviously, but I wish it would've happened tomorrow.

THOMAS: What is happening? What are we part of?

JOHN: Is it wrong to say I have no idea?

THOMAS: No, it makes me feel better.

RAMAH: I think I haven't had time to think about it. All this time, my parents I just know hate it. Other than that, I figured Thomas and I would get our answers from the rest of you.

THOMAS: The word is already spreading so fast … I didn't think about that. Have you thought about the fame from all this?

JOHN: I wouldn't mind being famous.

BIG JAMES: I'm not surprised.

PHILIP: It's not as fun as you might think.

JOHN: I cannot remember a time I didn't think about the Messiah at least once a week. My whole life I've prayed He'd come during this time, and I hoped I'd at least get to see Him. But to be close to Him like this? A nobody like me? What's not fun about that?

BIG JAMES: You call today fun?

PHILIP: Maybe not fun, but good. But with this fame comes enemies. You'll be hated too.

MATTHEW: I'm used to that.

PHILIP: Well, you were protected. And your enemies weren't powerful.

BIG JAMES: Speaking of enemies … if someone had told you growing up that you would be a student of the Messiah. YOU. You will be close to Him, you will help Him in His mission. What would you have thought?

RAMAH: I would have said, "Sorry, I'm a girl, ask my brother."

BIG JAMES: Fair enough. But really … Thomas, what would you have thought?

THOMAS: I would have thought, *I don't have military training.* That's still a problem, actually.

BIG JAMES: Exactly. When I was a child, I used to think how amazing it would be to see Messiah kill all the Romans on my street. And I even wanted to help Him, I trained every day with a wooden sword.

(John holds up his elbow.)

JOHN: Yes, and I have the scar that proves he was pretty good.

RAMAH: I used to imagine that the Romans would break into our home, and I would be hiding under the bed with a knife, and just when they came to get me, Messiah would rescue me at the last moment.

BIG JAMES: I didn't think we'd be spending our time healing—well, watching HIM heal. And they'll never stop, the people come, the more they hear about it and we're just going to be doing this the next five years and we'll never get around to the fighting part.

PHILIP: Eager to bring out that wooden sword of yours, are you?

All but Extinct

Meekness is a rare, misunderstood, and unadmired trait. Perhaps that's because the word *meek* rhymes with *weak*—and that's exactly what we think it means. We prefer adjectives like *bold, brave, impressive, fierce*. We pay attention to the people out front, the ones making names and taking names. We vote for strong political candidates, watch red-carpet award shows, and stand in line to get autographs from MVPs because we admire popular, wealthy, beautiful, successful, outspoken, and unabashed people.

And yet, blessed are the meek.

In a culture that puts self-protection, self-seeking, and self-empowerment above all else, meekness is a lost art. But contrary to Merriam-Webster, the Bible depicts being meek as having a quiet strength—one that's hidden beneath the surface, never wielded with recklessness or cruelty, but carefully deployed with gentle precision and thoughtfulness. A meek person isn't deficient in strength or courage; rather, he or she has chosen a posture of humility. Problem is, consistently putting others ahead of ourselves takes more strength than most of us actually have.

But more on that in a minute.

Your Turn

1. Be honest. Who do you admire and why? What are some of the characteristics that typically impress you most and that you most wish to possess? (Spoiler alert: meekness doesn't usually make the cut.)

THE MEEK 53

Little, Younger, Lesser

"There were also women looking on from a distance,
among whom were Mary Magdalene, and Mary the mother
of James the younger and of Joses, and Salome."
Mark 15:40

Two of Jesus's disciples shared the same name. James, son of Alphaeus, and James, son of Zebedee. Very little was written about James, son of Alphaeus, though he did score a nickname somewhere along the AD line: *James the Lesser*. You know, as opposed to *James the Greater*. Brutal, right? Some surmise the name was given as a result of his height; that he was the shorter of the two disciples. Some argue it was due to his age, that he was the younger of the two disciples. And some say it was due to the fact that he was less significant than "JAMES! SON OF THUNDER!" (… thunder! … thunder!), which begs the question: less significant according to whom?

What we do know is that "Little James" joined the One he believed would rescue the Jews (#bold). We know he trusted Jesus for daily provision of his basic needs, relinquishing the comfort and familiarity of home for the unpredictability, danger, and lack of comfort on the road (#brave). We know he submitted to Jesus's leadership, which included a whole lotta serving in spite of his personal lack (#impressive). And we know that after Jesus's death and resurrection, James and his fellow disciples took the gospel message to the ends of the earth, despite ongoing persecution and the likelihood of death (#fierce). We also know that in the New World he'll sit alongside Jesus on one of twelve thrones, judging the tribes of

For Bible Nerds (like us) Who Want to Know

"The Lesser" is used in 18 Bible translations.

"The Younger" is used in 32 Bible translations.

"The Little" is used in 2 Bible translations.

Language evolving over time leads to new translations, even within the same primary language (i.e., dozens of different English translations are available today). This is because there are several different ways to translate, including word for word, thought for thought, and paraphrasing.

Israel (Matt. 19:28), and that his name will be written on the very foundations of heaven (Rev. 21:14).

James the *Lesser*—ha! Only by our pathetic, shallow, sin-soaked human standards would James, son of Alphaeus, leader of the first-century church and personal friend to the Savior of the world, garner such a name. Then again, perhaps being called "lesser" was the best compliment he ever received.

Jesus actually chose those whom the world did not esteem—fishermen who were poor, a tax collector who was despised, a zealot who was radical and unruly, and women considered to be of lower standing than the men—to be on the ground floor of the kingdom He was bringing into the world. A kingdom with a very different set of priorities than what we humans deem important. And then Jesus preached accordingly, not only in the SOM, but also every day, in every way. He welcomed children, the poor, the sick, the outcast, and He taught His followers to serve them. Which means, like the depiction of the disciples in episode 3, we can be certain that Little James was sometimes surprised and confused by who Jesus was and what He chose to do. After all, the Jews were expecting the long-awaited Messiah to be a **not-meek** military leader who would set them free from the Roman occupation. Someone strong and powerful. Someone impressive to behold.

What they got instead changed everything.

For Bible Nerds (like us) Who Want to Know

The vision of the prophet in Zechariah 14 depicts a military action against Jerusalem and describes some of the horrors of war being conducted against the people there (vv. 1–2). While the date of the events depicted is not given, the Lord Himself is pictured as bringing victory over Jerusalem's enemies—and with earth-shattering effect (vv. 3–4). And so, it makes sense that some Jews were expecting the Messiah to come as a military victor to rescue His people from their enemies.

However, the astronomical and meteorological imagery (vv. 6–8), the descriptions of Jesus being "king over all the earth" (v. 9), and Jerusalem being forever safe from destruction (v. 11) confirm that the ultimate fulfillment of this prophecy will occur at the end of human history.

Your Turn

2. Meekness is an attitude of the heart, not a result of our DNA, our upbringing, or our inability to stand up for ourselves. According to Matthew 11:28–30, how do we adopt an attitude of meekness? Who is our example-in-chief?

3. It's been said that a meek person is not a weak person, but rather like a tamed lion—someone with "strength under control." How does that change the way you feel about the word? How does it change the way you might respond the next time you're mistreated?

4. God doesn't value what the world values. Underline the phrases below that describe the kind of people He chooses, and then explain why Little James had every reason to love and embrace his nickname.

"But God chose what is foolish in the world to shame the wise; God chose
what is weak in the world to shame the strong; God chose what is low
and despised in the world, even things that are not, to bring to nothing
things that are, so that no human being might boast in the presence of
God. And because of him you are in Christ Jesus, who became to us
wisdom from God, righteousness and sanctification and redemption,
so that, as it is written, 'Let the one who boasts, boast in the Lord.'"
1 Corinthians 1:27–35

The Other Side

"So [Jesus's] fame spread throughout all Syria, and they brought him all the sick, those afflicted with various diseases and pains, those oppressed by demons, those having seizures, and paralytics, and he healed them."

Matthew 4:24

The nation of Israel, which included the disciples, was indeed ready for a revolution. They'd been conquered and invaded by Rome—occupied, mistreated, and abused—and were therefore eagerly awaiting the promised Messiah, the One they believed would rescue and reinstate them in their homeland, the land given to their forefathers that they were supposed to inherit. Because *of course* that's what they assumed. They looked at their circumstances and couldn't imagine their Savior doing anything less. But while the followers of Jesus wanted an end to their suffering by way of war, what they got was the Sermon on the Mount and a whole new way of thinking, being, and responding.

"Love your enemies and pray for those who persecute you, so that you may be sons [and daughters] of your Father who is in heaven. For he makes his sun rise on the evil and on the good, and sends rain on the just and on the unjust. For if you

love those who love you, what reward do you have? Do not even the
tax collectors do the same? And if you greet only your brothers, what
more are you doing than others? Do not even the Gentiles do the same?
You therefore must be perfect, as your heavenly Father is perfect."

Matthew 5:44–48

Jesus spent His time healing and preaching about a future kingdom, not fighting and
reestablishing the present one. For that matter, He didn't engage in
social or political commentary at all, though both His followers
and enemies alike tried to get Him to. They raised issues of taxation
and tetrarchs, traditions and timelines because (like us) they
struggled to see beyond the moment they were living in. But Jesus
was focused on calling people to Himself, people who were broken
and humble and aware of their need for Him, because He saw

> "And if I go and prepare
> a place for you, I will
> come again and will take
> you to myself, that where
> I am you may be also."
> John 14:3

beyond who they were in that moment to who they would become by His healing, re-creating
hand. He saw beyond their circumstances to the place He would prepare for them.

Incidentally, moments by their very nature make us shortsighted and self-consumed
because there's nothing we *feel* more than the moments—including and especially ones
that induce anger, sadness, fear, defensiveness, or disappointment, all of which tempt us to
kick meekness to the curb. But Jesus's purpose was so much bigger than the moment. His
kingdom priorities were and are eternal, which is the whole reason He gathered followers
in the first place. Because when creation is finally restored and **eternity in all its
glory begins**, Jesus wants as many people with Him in it as possible.

Therefore, blessed are those who see beyond the moment—the ones who respond to
Jesus and then talk like Jesus and love like Jesus—because they get to be part of gathering
others to the kingdom! No wonder Jesus called His followers to be meek. Like Him, we're
enticing others to come with us, wooing them with the very patience, goodness, and
mercy that first drew us. And then someday soon we'll get to enjoy the fruit of that labor

as God's generosity toward us is poured out in a promised land so amazing our minds can't even comprehend it.

And that kind of knowledge should change everything. We choose meekness—we "deny ourselves" as our Savior did (Matt. 16:24–25)—*because of the promise.* Like James the Lesser, we make ourselves less by surrendering to Jesus as Lord the first day and all the days, knowing our inheritance is waiting for us on the other side of the moment. And because of God's faithfulness to carry us and enable us to do what He's asking us to do, He promised some other stuff too:

**Blessed are the meek because
they will be taken care of.**

"The wicked borrows but does not pay back, but the righteous is generous and gives; for those blessed by the LORD shall inherit the land."

Psalm 37:21–22

"You have heard that it was said, 'An eye for an eye and a tooth for a tooth.' But I say to you, Do not resist the one who is evil. But if anyone slaps you on the right cheek, turn to him the other also. And if anyone would sue you and take your tunic, let him have your cloak as well. And if anyone forces you to go one mile, go with him two miles. Give to the one who begs from you, and do not refuse the one who would borrow from you."

Matthew 5:38–42

"Therefore do not be anxious, saying, 'What shall we eat?' or 'What shall we drink?' or 'What shall we wear?' For the Gentiles seek after all these things, and your heavenly Father knows that you need them all. But seek first the kingdom of God and his righteousness, **and all these things will be added to you.**"
Matthew 6:31–33

"And everyone who has left houses or brothers or sisters or father or mother or children or lands, for my name's sake, will receive a hundredfold and will inherit eternal life. But many who are first will be last, **and the last first.**"
Matthew 19:29–30

Blessed are the meek because they will be lifted up.

"But you, O LORD, are a shield about me, my glory, and **the lifter of my head.**"
Psalm 3:3

"His mercy is for those who fear him from generation to generation. He has shown strength with his arm; he has scattered the proud in the thoughts of their hearts; he has brought down the mighty from their thrones and **exalted those of humble estate.**"
Luke 1:50–52

"Now he told a parable to those who were invited, when he noticed how they chose the places of honor, saying to them, 'When you are invited by someone to a wedding feast, do not sit down in a place of honor, lest someone more distinguished than you be invited by him, and he who invited you both will come and say to you, "Give your place to this person," and then you will begin with shame to take the lowest place. But when you are invited, go and sit in the lowest place, so that when your host comes he may say to you, "Friend, move up higher." Then you will be honored in the presence of all who sit at table with you. For everyone who exalts himself will be humbled, and he who humbles himself will be exalted.'"

Luke 14:7–11

"Clothe yourselves, all of you, with humility toward one another, for 'God opposes the proud but gives grace to the humble.'"

1 Peter 5:5

Blessed are the meek because they will be avenged.

"Fear not, stand firm, and see the salvation of the LORD, which he will work for you.... The LORD will fight for you, and you have only to be silent."

Exodus 14:13–14

"Do not say, 'I will repay evil'; wait for the LORD, and he will deliver you."

Proverbs 20:22

"And [Jesus] told them a parable to the effect that they ought always to pray and not lose heart. He said, 'In a certain city there was a judge who neither feared God nor respected man. And there was a widow in that city who kept coming to him and saying, "Give me justice against my adversary." For a while he refused, but afterward he said to himself, "Though I neither fear God nor respect man, yet because this widow keeps bothering me, I will give her justice, so that she will not beat me down by her continual coming."' And the Lord said, 'Hear what the unrighteous judge says. And will not God give justice to his elect, who cry to him day and night? Will he delay long over them? I tell you, he will give justice to them speedily.'"

Luke 18:1–8

"Repay no one evil for evil, but give thought to do what is honorable in the sight of all. If possible, so far as it depends on you, live peaceably with all. Beloved, never avenge yourselves, but leave it to the wrath of God, for it is written, 'Vengeance is mine, I will repay, says the Lord.' To the contrary, 'if your enemy is hungry, feed him; if he is thirsty, give him something to drink; for by so doing you will heap burning coals on his head.' Do not be overcome by evil, but overcome evil with good."

Romans 12:17–21

**Blessed are the meek because
they will be like Jesus.**

"Have this mind among yourselves, **which is yours in Christ Jesus**, who, though he was in the form of God, did not count equality with God a thing to be grasped, but emptied himself, by taking the form of a servant, being born in the likeness of men. And being found in human form, he humbled himself by becoming obedient to the point of death, even death on a cross. Therefore God has highly exalted him and bestowed on him the name that is above every name, so that at the name of Jesus every knee should bow, in heaven and on earth and under the earth, and every tongue confess that Jesus Christ is Lord, to the glory of God the Father."

Philippians 2:5–11

"For those whom he foreknew he also **predestined to be conformed to the image of his Son**, in order that he might be the firstborn among many brothers. And those whom he predestined he also called, and those whom he called he also justified, and those whom he justified he also glorified."

Romans 8:29–30

"For to this you have been called, because Christ also suffered for you, leaving you an example, so **that you might follow in his steps.** He committed no sin, neither was deceit found in his mouth. When he was reviled, he did not revile in return; when he suffered, he did not threaten, but continued entrusting himself to him who judges justly."

1 Peter 2:21–23

Your Turn

5. In light of the preceding verses, describe God's favor toward those who are meek.

6. Read Galatians 5:16–25. Where does our ability to choose meekness and self-control come from?

7. How does looking beyond the moment to your inheritance—the victory that is already yours in Jesus—change the way you see and handle the moment?

8. The surest way to maintain a spirit of meekness is to remember (a) you needed to be saved, (b) God saved you, and (c) where you're going as a result. Read Ephesians 2:5–7, and then briefly write out your own testimony, making special mention of God's mercy and the promise of your inheritance.

THOMAS: I don't get it, if I'm honest. I don't know why God has allowed the occupation. I'd love to ask Him *(indicates toward Jesus)* more about that, why this has been allowed for so long. It's hard to feel like the chosen people.

SIMON: I've been there.

RAMAH: But it's worth it now, yes? The wait is over.

(Thomas nods and smiles. Simon looks at Matthew, who has been silent this whole time.)

SIMON: What about you?

MATTHEW: What do you mean?

SIMON: Has it been difficult for you? All this time? The occupation, following Jewish law?

MATTHEW: My life has not been easy.

SIMON: Oh, it hasn't? What was more painful for you—escaping Roman persecution by working for them, or escaping your guilt with all the money? And now you're catching up on Torah and wanting to follow the law? Why now, all of a sudden? Why not all the other times you've had the chance?

JOHN: Simon.

SIMON: No, no, John, I want to know … Mary had horrible trauma, she didn't choose all that happened to her. What's your excuse?

MATTHEW: What do you want me to say? I don't know what you want from me.

ANDREW: An apology.

MATTHEW: What?

(Mary Mother and Little James emerge from the trees and stop, watching.)

ANDREW: Simon's not wrong. He could be more delicate about it, but you did choose to work for them, and you made my life even harder than it already was, and you haven't apologized. *(Matthew opens his mouth to speak.)*

SIMON: No—no—don't say it, I don't want you to apologize, it doesn't matter. What will hearing him say he's sorry do? I won't forgive it anyway.

JOHN: What keeps putting you in authority? Who are you to forgive or not to forgive?

SIMON: What, you're on his side?

JOHN: No, of course not! But you've had your problems too! What about apologizing for what you almost did to us with the Romans?

SIMON: I didn't go through with it! I was trying to save my family's life, and I love you, John, but that's not something you have to worry about when Zeb and Salome are looking out for you. *(to Matthew)* But you put me in a desperate position where I did things I would NEVER have done otherwise, and I've repented for them, and John and James, I am sorry, but I didn't go through with it.

THOMAS *(to Matthew)*: What IS your excuse? I was a successful businessman, and yet I was always behind.

JOHN: He wasn't your tax collector.

THOMAS: Quit defending him, I want an answer!

BIG JAMES *(stands up)*: Hey! You're new—

SIMON: Do you even know what it's like to be Jewish? To suffer for centuries and centuries because of it but to still commit to it? To protect our heritage even though it never stops being painful, because the ONE COMFORT we have is to know that we're doing it TOGETHER? That we're all suffering together, but if we just wait a little longer, if we hold tight just a little more, we'll have rescue, because we're chosen? All of us! And you betrayed that, and you spit on it! I can't forgive it! I'll never forgive it!

BIG JAMES: All right, you've said what you needed to say. Sit down, Simon.

ANDREW *(standing up to defend his brother)*: You sit down first!

(A noise from the trees stops them. They look over … it's Jesus. He's moving slowly, shoulders slumped, every muscle weakened. There's blood on Him from the people He's been healing. His wrinkled clothes are drenched in sweat and hanging. He shuffles past.)

JESUS *(in a whisper)*: Good night.

(Jesus stops at His tent. He's barely able to stand, hands shaky. Mary Mother walks quickly to Him. She helps take off His cloak.)

JESUS: Oh, *Eema* … thank you.

(She removes His sandals, washes His feet. Then His hands. Some disciples watch, others hang their heads.)

MARY MOTHER: You've got blood on Your hands *(wiping Jesus's forehead)*. One more … there we go.

JESUS: I'm a mess. Good?

MARY MOTHER: Good.

JESUS *(kissing her on the head)*: What would I do without you, *Eema*?

MARY MOTHER: Get some sleep.

JESUS: Okay. I'm so tired.

(He lies down in bed. As Mary arranges His things, we faintly hear the beginning of His bedtime prayer.)

JESUS (CONT'D): "Blessed are You, Lord our God, King of the Universe, who brings sleep to my eyes and slumber to my eyelids. May it be Your will, Lord my God and God of my ancestors, that I lie down in peace and that I arise in peace …"

(On the disciples in silence as we … CUT TO BLACK.)

Prayer Focus

Contemplate the places or issues in your life where, like some of the disciples in episode 3, you would like a little justice for the ways you've been wronged … or at least an acknowledgment from others that you've been wronged and an apology for the hurt they've caused. Talk to the Lord about your feelings and about the people involved. Thank Him for understanding the pain of those circumstances, and ask Him for wisdom to know what to do: to overlook the offense without being irritable (Prov. 19:11; 1 Cor. 13:4–7), to engage in loving confrontation and forgiveness (Matt. 18:15–22; Luke 17:3–4),

To be meek does not mean to tolerate or remain in an abusive relationship. If you're being abused, seek help. It's not God's will for you to be abused. Again, meek doesn't mean weak.

and/or to seek the counsel and assistance of trusted Christian advisers (1 Pet. 5:1–5; Gal. 6:1–3). Ask God to empower you by His Holy Spirit with the courage and strength to do it all with an attitude of meekness.

Sample Prayer

Dear Lord,

You know everything, including when I'm frustrated or hurt or I'm being overlooked. I acknowledge that I have not always responded with the proper meekness. Forgive me for the places where I've been thinking only of myself—of my own pain, embarrassment, and shame—and for where I may be desiring an inordinate level of justice. Even vengeance.

Help me to think clearly and rightly and wisely, Lord. Help me to let go of petty grudges and, when necessary, with loving confrontation, to offer forgiveness instead of seeking revenge. You have given me so much to be grateful for, and I trust that You have even more for me ahead. For all of that I give You thanks.

Amen.

Simon the Zealot

The second of the apostles with the name Simon is distinguished from Simon Peter, not by adding a second name, but by adding a note about his political leanings (i.e., his affiliation with the Zealots [Luke 6:15; Acts 1:13]). The Zealots were part of an anti-Roman movement among first-century Jews, so Simon the Zealot is noted for his passion against the Roman occupation in the land of Israel. In a few translations he is referred to as "Simon the Cananaean," where the label "Cananaean" stems from a transliteration of the Aramaic word for "Zealot."

Little is known about this apostle, and various traditions about him sometimes confuse and conflate with stories about Jesus's brother named Simon (which also happened with James and Judas because they too shared names with Jesus's brothers [Matt. 13:55; Mark 6:3]). Records indicate that Simon the Zealot had a ministry in Parthia (the region of ancient Persia and modern Iran), parts of which were in partnership with Judas Thaddaeus (a.k.a., Jude). With his new zeal for Jesus, Simon the Zealot is thought to have also carried the gospel message to parts of Africa (Egypt and Mauritania), Lydia (a region of modern-day Turkey), and possibly even to Britain. Variously represented in the legends, Simon the Zealot was martyred in Parthia by being beaten (with sticks and stones and/or with swords and spears), crucified, and/or sawn in half (AD 72). Interestingly, among the legends about the apostles, Simon the Zealot and Thaddaeus are the only two of the original disciples to die together in any story.

Lesson 4

THOSE WHO HUNGER
and the ones who cease

"Blessed are those who hunger and thirst for righteousness, for they shall be satisfied."

Matthew 5:6

EXT. POOL OF BETHESDA (AFTERNOON)

SIMON Z: I can't believe it. You're worse than you used to be.

JESSE: My legs are the same as when you left.

SIMON Z: I'm not talking about your legs, I'm talking about you. This Godforsaken place has turned my strong brother into someone hopeless.

JESSE: And what should I hope in after all these years? You and your murderous kind?

SIMON Z: Jesse, it's killed me to watch you suffer in your life, and I'm sorry, I truly am. But that's not the only kind of pain, and you're not the only one who feels it. But you know what? I'm at least doing something about mine, and I'm not sitting on a bed waiting to die.

JESSE *(looking down)*: Have you said all you need to say?

SIMON Z: I have to be in the Upper City.

JESSE: That's nearby. Less than a mile away. Might as well be a thousand miles to me. *(crying)* Whoever it is, don't do it. It's not worth it. If they catch you, they'll kill you!

SIMON Z: I'm not afraid of death.

(Jesse's heart breaks at the words.)

SIMON Z (CONT'D): I just wanted to say goodbye, because I didn't do it right the first time. I do love you. And I love God. Goodbye, Jesse.

(As Simon Z turns to go, Jesse pulls out the letter Simon had written years before.)

JESSE: "… by the time you read this, I will be halfway to the mountains, to join the Zealots of the Fourth Philosophy, in the spirit of our great King David who sang: 'Zeal for your house has consumed me.'"

SIMON Z: My note. I was a better writer then.

JESSE: "And from Zephaniah, 'Behold, at that time I will deal with all your oppressors. And I will save the lame and gather the outcast; I will change their shame into praise and renown in all the earth.' Jesse, when you stand on two feet, I will know the Messiah has come. I will fight for the freedom of Zion in order to see that day."

(The words hang in the air. Simon Z turns back briefly to his brother.)

SIMON Z: I stand by it. Farewell, Jesse.

Pools and Such

Sometimes we seek the right things in the wrong places. Sometimes we seek the wrong things for the right reasons. Sometimes we seek the wrong things in the wrong places because we long to fill the void in our hearts—to restore what was once right despite our total inability to do so. And sometimes, by the grace of God, we seek the right thing in the right place.

And then we find.

But let's not get ahead of ourselves because we live in a deeply unsatisfying world—which is strange considering we have more choices, more conveniences, and more comforts than at any other point in history. Such advancements and general prosperity (think electricity, refrigeration, plumbing, cars, planes, etc.) should've secured our contentment. But the opposite is true, and by and large, humanity is unsettled and unfulfilled.

Why is that? Well, social media, for starters. Every day we have access to platforms that are constantly being updated with everyone's best thing—pictures of vacations, beautiful food, good hair days, well-behaved families, and videos that make it seem like absolutely everyone can dance. But back in reality where we actually live, nothing is perfect and happiness is fleeting. We might get the job, the house, the car, the relationship, or the acknowledgment we're longing for, but every new thing comes with its own set of problems. And as it turns out, having more choices, along with access to seeing *other* people's choices, creates greater discontentment, not less, because there's always more to do, see, be, have, and experience.

Truth is, **nothing apart from God actually satisfies**—not really, not permanently, not completely—because He created us to *only* be satisfied in Him.

He's smart like that.

Your Turn

1. What are some things you assumed would bring you contentment and satisfaction? Did they? Why, or why not?

What's in a Name?

"[Jesus] called to him his twelve disciples and gave them authority
over unclean spirits, to cast them out, and to heal every disease and
every affliction. The names of the twelve apostles are these: first,
Simon, who is called Peter, and Andrew his brother; James the son of

Zebedee, and John his brother; Philip and Bartholomew; Thomas and
Matthew the tax collector; James the son of Alphaeus, and Thaddaeus;
Simon the Zealot, and Judas Iscariot, who betrayed him."
Matthew 10:1–5

The Zealots were a fiercely militant sect of Judaism whose members carried out assassinations on both Roman leaders *and* Jewish leaders whom they believed were either (1) collaborating with Rome's occupation of the land or (2) accommodating Rome's demands too readily. And Simon Z was fresh off the death-squad boat, which is why his name became a phrase: Simon the Zealot.

How would you like to be remembered throughout history for the person you were right *before* you met Jesus? Of course you wouldn't want that, and neither did the other disciples since it would've gone something like this: Mary of Magdala the Demonic, Matthew the Taxman Traitor, Nathanael the Rude and Kinda Racist, Simon Peter the Oft Emotionally Unstable—you get the idea. No, generally speaking, we don't memorialize our "befores," because that part of the story typically gets swallowed up by God's forgiveness, redemption, and grace. It's intentionally forgotten by God. And then as we follow Jesus, we become more like Him and less like the *before* we once were.

But Simon Z's before serves an interesting purpose because, generally speaking, the Zealots actually longed for some right things. They wanted to see Israel restored and the Messiah, God's Chosen One, on His throne and ruling with justice for all. They wanted intimacy with God. They were zealous for Him, for freedom, and for a return to the way things were created to be—which were all good things. Unfortunately, the Zealots were

> "I, I am he who blots out your transgressions for my own sake, and I will not remember your sins."
> Isaiah 43:25

> "He does not deal with us according to our sins, nor repay us according to our iniquities. For as high as the heavens are above the earth, so great is his steadfast love toward those who fear him; as far as the east is from the west, so far does he remove our transgressions from us."
> Psalm 103:10–12

also sin-soaked, misguided, and just plain wrong in their interpretation of Scripture—which were all not good things.

Yet, blessed are those who hunger and thirst for righteousness. Blessed are those who seek. Blessed are those who long for God's proper place in the hearts of men and women to be restored. And blessed was Simon the Zealot, who longed for a right thing in a wrong place but was mercifully still chosen and *made right* by the only One who could.

> Righteousness:
> right standing before God.

> "Ask, and it will be given to you; seek, and you will find; knock, and it will be opened to you. For everyone who asks receives, and the one who seeks finds, and to the one who knocks it will be opened."
> Matthew 7:7–8

Your Turn

2. What does it mean to hunger and thirst for righteousness?

> "And the King will answer them, 'Truly, I say to you, as you did it to one of the least of these my brothers, you did it to me.'"
> Matthew 25:40

3. Imagine Simon Z's early days with Jesus: a brave, reckless, passionate, and angry young man spending hours on end with the promised Messiah he'd been waiting for. Yet, rather than satisfying Simon's thirst for revenge against the Romans or his longing to see

For Bible Nerds (like us) Who Want to Know

Several places in Scripture use the imagery of hunger and thirst to describe our desire for the things of God:

"As a deer pants for flowing streams, so pants my soul for you, O God. My soul thirsts for God, for the living God" (Ps. 42:1–2); "O God, you are my God; earnestly I seek you; my soul thirsts for you; my flesh faints for you, as in a dry and weary land where there is no water" (Ps. 63:1); "I will send a famine on the land—not a famine of bread, nor a thirst for water, but of hearing the words of the LORD" (Amos 8:11).

Israel reinstated as a free, self-ruling nation in the Promised Land, Jesus enlisted Simon to listen and learn and serve the least of these.

That's all … just imagine.

4. Read the verses below and underline the ways we can pursue righteousness, taking special notice of what it says about our behavior toward others (which, for the record, includes our behavior on social media platforms).

> "Flee youthful passions and pursue righteousness, faith, love, and peace, along with those who call on the Lord from a pure heart. Have nothing to do with foolish, ignorant controversies; you know that they breed quarrels. And the Lord's servant must not be quarrelsome but kind to everyone, able to teach, patiently enduring evil, correcting his opponents with gentleness. God may perhaps grant them repentance leading to a knowledge of the truth, and they may come to their senses and escape from the snare of the devil, after being captured by him to do his will."
> 2 Timothy 2:22–26

Enter Jesus

> "Now there is in Jerusalem by the Sheep Gate a pool, in Aramaic called Bethesda, which has five roofed colonnades. In these lay a multitude of invalids—blind, lame, and paralyzed. One man was there who had been an invalid for thirty-eight years. When Jesus saw him lying there and knew that he had already been there a long time, he said to him, 'Do you want to be healed?' The sick man answered him, 'Sir, I have no one to put me into the pool when the water is stirred up, and while I am going another steps down before me.' Jesus said to him, 'Get up, take up your bed, and walk.' And at once the man was healed, and he took up his bed and walked."
> John 5:2–9

While the Zealots were warring, Simon Z was watching because Jesus was setting his kinsmen free in a way he could never have imagined. Yes, the lame were made to walk and the blind were made to see, but Jesus was also ushering in a whole new kind of peace—a spiritual healing that eclipsed even the hostility of the Roman occupation. Like the man at the pool of Bethesda, Simon had been looking for a right thing in a wrong place. But that didn't stop Jesus from entering in.

"Do you want to be healed?"

What a strange question, because of course the guy did. Every person with a physical affliction in that place wanted to be healed; it's why they were there. But no one seemed to take notice of the One who was *actually* able to heal them. Jesus walked among them—the sick and diseased, the deaf, blind, and lame—while they focused their time and energy and hope on the water. Which should sound familiar, because we do the same thing. We humans focus on the things we think will make us happy, the things we've decided we need in this life, while Jesus freely offers us the very satisfaction and peace our hearts are longing for.

Simon hungered for good things—for personal righteousness and for God's people to be restored in their own land with the Messiah as their king. But then he met Jesus, who was the answer to all those things, which is why Simon the Zealot became Simon the Satisfied, having his desires and pursuits reordered and transformed by the One he was following. And the result was a quieting contentment found nowhere else on earth.

Not in a political party.

Not in money.

Not in relationships.

Not in accomplishments or accolades or Instalikes.

Not in good health or a long life.

Only in Jesus.

And that kind of knowledge should change everything. Of course, ultimate righteousness—the kind where good forevermore prevails over evil—will eventually be found in the consummated kingdom of God, which He will bring about in His timing and in His way; that is, with the second coming of Jesus. (#ComeQuicklyLord … cuz things are a mess down here!) But in the meantime, blessed are those who hunger and thirst for God and His righteousness because **they will be satisfied** in the here and now and in the by and by:

Consummated: to complete; to make perfect.

"For the Lord himself will descend from heaven with a cry of command, with the voice of an archangel, and with the sound of the trumpet of God. And the dead in Christ will rise first. Then we who are alive, who are left, will be caught up together with them in the clouds to meet the Lord in the air, and so we will always be with the Lord."
1 Thessalonians 4:16–17

Satisfaction in Jesus

=

No more searching

"And the Word became flesh and dwelt among us, **and we have seen his glory**, glory as of the only Son from the Father, full of grace and truth."

John 1:14

For Bible Nerds (like us) Who Want to Know

"The Word" = Jesus Christ

Both Genesis and the Psalms tell us that God spoke the world into being (Gen. 1; Ps. 33).

John later wrote his gospel in Greek, which is a language that uses "word" ("logos") to describe divine reason and

that which gives the world form and meaning; the eternal organizing principle of existence itself.

So it makes sense that John merged these two ideas by using the colorful term "Word" for Christ, who has always existed and was present for the creation of the world.

"Jesus said to them, 'I am the bread of life; whoever comes to me shall not hunger, and whoever believes in me shall never thirst.'"

John 6:35

"Jesus said to him, 'I am the way, and the truth, and the life. No one comes to the Father except through me.'"

John 14:6

"And there is salvation in no one else, for there is no other name under heaven given among men by which we must be saved."

Acts 4:12

Satisfaction in Jesus

=

No more striving for things that vanish, fade, rot, and rust

"Lift up your eyes to the heavens, and look at the earth beneath; for the heavens vanish like smoke, the earth will wear out like a garment, and they who dwell in it will die in like manner; but my salvation will be forever, and my righteousness will never be dismayed."

Isaiah 51:6

Dismayed: wane, fade, fail.

"Jesus said to her, 'Everyone who drinks of this water will be thirsty again, but whoever drinks of the water that I will give him will never be thirsty again. The water that I will give him will become in him a spring of water welling up to eternal life.'"

John 4:13–14

"Do not lay up for yourselves treasures on earth, where moth and rust destroy and where thieves break in and steal, but lay up for yourselves treasures in heaven, where neither moth nor rust destroys and where thieves do not break in and steal. For where your treasure is, there your heart will be also."

Matthew 6:19–21

"Heaven and earth will pass away, but my words will not pass away."

Mark 13:31

Satisfaction in Jesus
=
Continual refreshment

"And the LORD will guide you continually and satisfy your desire in scorched places and make your bones strong; and you shall be like a watered garden, like a spring of water, whose waters do not fail."

Isaiah 58:11

"I will restore to you the years that the swarming locust has eaten, the hopper, the destroyer, and the cutter, my great army, which I sent among you. You shall eat in plenty and be satisfied, and praise the name of the LORD your God, who has dealt wondrously with you. And my people shall never again be put to shame."

Joel 2:25–26

"Come to me, all who labor and are heavy laden, and **I will give you rest**. Take my yoke upon you, and learn from me, for I am gentle and lowly in heart, and **you will find rest for your souls**. For my yoke is easy, and my burden is light."

Matthew 11:28–30

"Therefore, if anyone is in Christ, he is a new creation. The old has passed away; **behold, the new has come**."

2 Corinthians 5:17

Satisfaction in Jesus

Hope and joy in spite of the chaos

"You make known to me the path of life; **in your presence there is fullness of joy**; at your right hand are pleasures forevermore."

Psalm 16:11

"Peace I leave with you; my peace I give to you. Not as the world gives do I give to you. **Let not your hearts be troubled, neither let them be afraid**."

John 14:27

"May the God of hope fill you with all joy and peace in believing, so that by the power of the Holy Spirit you may **abound in hope**."

Romans 15:13

Your Turn

5. In light of the preceding verses, describe God's favor toward those who hunger and thirst for righteousness.

6. Read 2 Peter 3:11–13, then answer the question it asks:

"What sort of people ought you to be?" (Hint, hint … the answer is in verse 13.)

7. How would "waiting for and hastening the coming of the day of God" change the way you see and respond to the culture, to your circumstances, and to your earthly hopes and dreams, whether realized or not?

8. Even after we come to Jesus, we can thwart His favor in our lives. In what ways are you refusing God's peace and soul satisfaction? Maybe the better question is:

Do you want to be healed?

EXT. POOL OF BETHESDA

(The area is notably quiet for the Sabbath. Jesus and three others approach the sandstone pool.)

SIMON: This is what all the fuss is about? An oversized *mikveh*?

JOHN: I have a feeling we haven't seen it all yet.

(As they descend the stairs, a troubling vision sprawls out before them. Bodies broken, lame, deformed. People in the final stages of terminal illness. Lepers. Oh, the lepers. Many unable to move on their own. Matthew covers his nose. Jesus takes in the sight. He is unsurprised by the sight but still moved. Among the helpless, hopeless, mostly immobile group of sufferers, Jesus spots Jesse.)

JESUS: That's him.

SIMON: Who?

JESUS: Him. The one who's been here the longest but doesn't belong. The sad one.

SIMON: Why do I get the feeling this isn't just a meeting? Do we need to be on the lookout?

JESUS: No. Just stay with Me and watch.

(He approaches Jesse.)

JESUS (CONT'D): Shalom.

JESSE *(seeing Jesus standing above him)*: Me?

(John and Matthew glance at each other and smirk.)

JESUS: Yes.

JESSE: Shalom.

JESUS: I have a question for you.

(The invalid looks up, intrigued.)

JESSE: For me? *(Jesus stares.)* I don't have many answers, but … I'm listening.

JESUS: Do you want to be healed?

JESSE *(confused)*: Who are You?

JESUS: We'll get to that later. But my question remains.

JESSE *(hopeful)*: Will You take me to the water?

(Jesus shakes His head.)

JESSE (CONT'D): Look, I'm having a really bad day.

JESUS: You've been having a bad day for a long time. So?

JESSE: Sir, I have no one to help me into the water when it's stirred up, and when I do get close … the others step down in front of me. And so—

JESUS *(kneeling down, eye to eye)*: Look at Me. Look at Me. That's not what I asked. I'm not asking you about who's helping you or who's not helping, or who's getting in your way … I'm asking about you.

JESSE *(tears form)*: I've tried.

JESUS: For a long time, I know. And you don't want false hope again, I understand. But this pool has nothing for you; it means nothing and you know it. But you're still here. Why?

JESSE *(whispers)*: I don't know.

JESUS: You don't need this pool. You only need Me. So … do you want to be healed?

(Jesse looks into his eyes … tears escalate. He doesn't need to say yes.)

JESUS: So let's go. Get up, pick up your mat, and walk.

Prayer Focus

Talk to God about the things you find yourself hungering and thirsting for. Ask the Lord to forgive you for the times you've sought good or right things in wrong ways or places. Thank Him for providing for all of your needs and offering you a purpose-driven life following Him. Ask Him to empower you by His Holy Spirit to hunger and thirst for righteousness so completely that you'd seek it in the right ways and in the right places—and that you'd grow to ultimately seek Him alone.

Sample Prayer

Dear Lord,

I find within myself a strong desire to make a difference in the world. Even if it's a small impact, I want my life to have significance and to influence others for good. But I admit that sometimes my competing desires get in the way. Please forgive me. I'm grateful for Your conviction and guidance to keep me moving toward You and the things You care about. May Your Holy Spirit work in me to desire right things so that I find my satisfaction, significance, rest, and hope in You.

Amen.

First-Century Religious Leaders in Judaism

The *temple* was Judaism's official worship center where the priests conducted various sacrifices and ceremonies outlined for Old Testament Israel. It was the domain of the Levites and the priesthood. The *Levites*—descendants from the Israelite tribe of Levi—served in various roles as assistants to the Jewish priesthood. The *priests*, who led temple worship activities, were also Levites but from a specific branch of Aaron's descendants. Aaron, Moses's brother, served as Israel's first *high priest* (Ex. 28).

While the Jerusalem temple was the domain of the priesthood, the local *synagogues* were for everyday people to study Scripture and pray without making the long journey to the Jerusalem temple. With the Levitical leadership engaged in the official temple system, the leadership of local synagogues often fell to laypeople: Sadducees and Pharisees.

Of uncertain origin, the first-century party of the *Sadducees* tended to more readily accept Roman rule. Content with the way things were, this group held the Pentateuch (the five books written by Moses) to be the most authoritative Scripture and were not looking for a messianic figure to rise up and rescue the Jews. Sadducees also denied life after death, physical resurrection, and spiritual beings (Matt. 22:23; Mark 12:18; Luke 20:27; Acts 23:8).

Readers of the New Testament may be surprised to learn that the *Pharisees* were often well-intentioned people interested in applying the Bible to their everyday lives. The Pharisees were highly respected Bible believers who held to the whole of the Hebrew Scriptures as God's Word and who desired to maintain a life of purity by properly observing the Law. Unlike the Sadducees, they affirmed life after death, physical resurrection, and spiritual beings (Acts 23:8). It's important to note that Jesus's complaint against the Pharisees was not so much about their goal of holy living but rather their hypocritical way of favoring their own oral traditions (man-made rules) over the actual intent of the written Law (Matt. 15:1–20; 23:1–36; Mark 7:1–23; Luke 11:37–54).

Rome understood the importance of faith to the Jews, so they allowed the Jews a degree of cultural self-governance by way of the *Sanhedrin*, the highest Jewish council. In the New Testament era, the Sanhedrin consisted of seventy-one leaders and priests with the Jewish high priest as its ultimate leader. Within the limits granted by Rome, this group exercised wide-ranging oversight of Jewish legal and religious concerns. While Sanhedrin members could be Sadducees or Pharisees, in the New Testament era the Sadducees dominated the council (Acts 4:1–22; 5:17–27). Of course, as with any human institution (including those with religious purposes), the Sanhedrin could be subject to sinful influences and corrupt motivations.

Okay, that's it … because that was probably more information on first-century religious leaders in Judaism than you ever wanted to know.

Lesson 5

THE MERCIFUL
and their mandate

"Blessed are the merciful, for they shall receive mercy."

Matthew 5:7

INT. JERUSALEM TEMPLE (CHAMBER OF OILS)

(In the Chamber of Oils within the temple courts, Yanni and Shmuel interrogate a recently healed Jesse. As if repeating the question—)

YANNI: Did He tell you His name?!

JESSE: Jesus.

YANNI: Jesus who? From where?

SHMUEL: Lineage? Origin?

JESSE *(sarcastically)*: His favorite food? He told me His name. That's it.

YANNI: There were a million Jews here for the festival, thousands named Jesus.

SHMUEL: Jesse, stop pacing.

JESSE: With all due respect, Rabbi, I've been still for thirty-eight years.

YANNI: Tell us exactly what He said. *(off Jesse's look)* Again!

JESSE: He told me to go and sin no more, that the result of sin is far worse than being crippled.

YANNI: And to pick up your mat.

JESSE *(after a beat)*: When He healed me, yes. But He found me earlier today as well.

SHMUEL: Was anyone with Him?

JESSE *(searching his memory)*: Three men? One was taking notes. I think another said a few words to me as Jesus disappeared. I barely heard anything—my LEGS!

(Jesse trails off, lost in the memory, reverie.)

SHMUEL: Jesse?

JESSE *(back to the present)*: The other said something. But by the time you finished yelling at me, they were all gone.

SHMUEL: Think! What did he say to you today?

(Jesse racks his brain. Then, uncertain—)

JESSE: They were going to see Jesus's … cousin? I think.

(Shmuel turns to Yanni with urgency.)

SHMUEL: It was Him. It was Jesus of Nazareth.

Religiosity

Fancy robes and head coverings definitely set religious leaders apart. The pope is perhaps the most recognizable, but there are also imams, lamas, pujaris, and priests. When they're dressed for work, you can see these guys coming a mile away, because they wear their ideas about life on their proverbial sleeves. Wait, no, on their literal sleeves.

Far less obvious are the pious people in street clothes. Though many are sincere in their belief, like the fictional character of Shmuel, they major in the minors. They hyper-focus on outward behavior—on rules, regulations, and rituals—while neglecting the inside. But religion apart from Jesus has a way of hardening our hearts and calcifying our hidden sins like pride, self-centeredness, judgmentalism, and unforgiveness—just to name a few. Not to mention the damage such religiosity does to the very people Jesus came to save, but more on them in a minute.

Religion = humanity's attempt to reach God.

Relationship with Jesus = God's attempt to reach humanity.

Truth is, it doesn't take a black robe to be a Shmuel. By our very nature, we judge others harshly, hold on to grievances, and sometimes even cease to associate with people we deem unworthy of our time or attention—and oftentimes in the name of religion. Which for Christians is wholly ironic, considering it was our desperate need for God's mercy that drew us to Him in the first place.

Your Turn

1. In what ways are you a Shmuel?

Lest you think
Matthew 23:23 doesn't
apply to you ...

Hypocrisy:
claiming to have moral
standards or beliefs to
which one's own behavior
does not always conform.

Selective Memory

"Woe to you, scribes and Pharisees, hypocrites! For you tithe mint and dill and cumin, and have neglected the weightier matters of the law: justice and mercy and faithfulness. These you ought to have done, without neglecting the others."

Matthew 23:23

Which means every human
in the history of humans
has been a hypocrite at
one time or another.

Tithe:
one-tenth of a person's
produce or earnings.

The fifth Beatitude of the SOM marks a slight change in direction. The first four blessed statements focus on <u>individual transformation</u> resulting from God's work and favor in our lives. The last four focus on our <u>interaction with others</u> resulting from God's work and favor in our lives—starting with being merciful. Remarkably, the only other New Testament use of this particular adjective is a description of Jesus in Hebrews 2:17: "Therefore he had to be made like his brothers in every respect, so that he might become a merciful and faithful high priest in the service of God, to make propitiation for the sins of the people." As God's chosen

Propitiation:
appeasing God; to atone.

Atone:
to make amends.

Amends:
just kidding ... we'll
stop now since you
can just google if you
don't know a word.

people **and as a result of His favor toward us**, we become more like Jesus as we follow Him. Which means by His mercy, He's making us merciful.

> "How can you say to your brother, 'Let me take the speck out of your eye,' when there is the LOG in your own eye?"
>
> Matthew 7:4

That said, there was a sad and great divide between the way Jesus treated people and the way many of the religious leaders of His day treated people. Time and again, they prioritized public religious actions (praying, tithing, sacrificing) ahead of private, personal *inter*actions—with God and with fellow believers. They were more concerned with being seen, honored, and set apart (Matt. 23:1–12) than they were with matters of the heart, first and foremost their own. They were more likely to punish when people broke the rules than they were to show

God's rules = the Ten Commandments

mercy when people repented. Incidentally, God's rules were given out of love. They were intended for our good—to act as guardrails that protect, lead, and keep us close to Him and to one another. But in the hands of sinful men, God's laws became cudgels of power used to elevate some and shame others. To wield God's *way* like a hammer.

Religion like that doesn't woo people. It repels them.

Ironically, showing mercy is an outward indication of a person's right relationship with God, because "out of the abundance of the heart his mouth speaks" (Luke 6:45).

> "None is righteous, no, not one."
>
> Romans 3:10

Like Shmuel's, our hearts and priorities get all discombobulated, especially when we forget how much we've been forgiven. We judge others quickly, ignorantly, and harshly. We carelessly throw our words around, or we withhold kind words. We act like we're good when the

For Bible Nerds (like us) Who Want to Know

The noun form of *mercy* is more common in the New Testament (used 27 times). And in Matthew's Gospel, Jesus expresses God's high valuation of mercy and His intention to convey mercy to humanity:

"Go and learn what this means: 'I desire mercy, and not sacrifice.' For I came not to call the righteous, but sinners" (Matt. 9:13, citing Hos. 6:6).

"And if you had known what this means, 'I desire mercy, and not sacrifice,' you would not have condemned the guiltless" (Matt. 12:7, citing Hos. 6:6).

truth is we're not, and instead of testifying of God's mercy and the changes He's made in our lives, we attempt to glorify ourselves. But when we take a moment to remember His great mercy toward us, **and we operate from a proper place of humility**, we begin to interact with people in a whole new way.

After all, as the saying goes:

The ground at the foot of the cross is level.

Your Turn

2. What are some of the ways God has shown you mercy?

3. When do you most often fail to show mercy, and why? Be brave by being honest and specific.

4. Read Matthew 5:43–48 and Luke 6:32–36. According to these verses, who are you supposed to show mercy to? And more to the point, what excuse do you have for failing to show mercy?

High Priest

"Therefore the kingdom of heaven may be compared to a king who wished to settle accounts with his servants. When he began to settle, one was brought to him who owed him ten thousand talents. And since he could not pay, his master ordered him to be sold, with his wife and children and all that he had, and payment to be made. So the servant fell on his knees, imploring him, 'Have patience with me, and I will pay you everything.' And out of pity for him, **the master of that servant released him and forgave him the debt.** But when that same servant went out, he found one of his fellow servants who owed him a hundred denarii, and seizing him, he began to choke him, saying, 'Pay what you owe.' So his fellow servant fell down and pleaded with him, 'Have patience with me, and I will pay you.' He refused and went and put him in prison until he should pay the debt. When his fellow servants saw what had taken place, they were greatly distressed, and they went and reported to their master all that had taken place. Then his master summoned him and said to him, 'You wicked servant! I forgave you all that debt because you pleaded with me. And should not you have had mercy on your fellow servant, as I had mercy on you?' And in anger his master delivered him to the jailers, until he should pay all his debt. So also my heavenly Father will do to every one of you, if you do not forgive your brother from your heart."

Matthew 18:23–35

"Do not be deceived: God is not mocked, for whatever one sows, that will he also reap. For the one who sows to his own flesh will from the flesh reap corruption, but the one who sows to the Spirit will from the Spirit reap eternal life."

Galatians 6:7–8

Yikes. In a Bible study about God's favor being presently, generously, and eternally poured upon His chosen people, Matthew 18:35 hits hard—which is a good thing, lest we forget Who we're dealing with. Because while it's true that

God is merciful toward us—that He forgives those who repent, that He carries us forward, and that His love extends beyond what our minds can even comprehend—it's also true that His mercy **is not to be trifled with.**

Blessed are the merciful, for they shall receive mercy; that's true and hallelujah! But according to the parable Jesus told in Matthew 18, woe to those who are *not* merciful, because **the day is coming when we will face the God of mercy and justice.** And just like a parent motivates a child with rewards and consequences, so too does our heavenly Father. Want to continually receive mercy? Give mercy, because God's children receive it in endless doses for the purpose of spreading it around. It's a free gift *and* a promised reward. Also true? Withhold mercy and God will withhold mercy from you.

Those who follow Jesus are broken but redeemed people, and therefore greatly favored. And that kind of knowledge should change everything. Those chosen by God have experienced His mercy, and we're going to keep on experiencing it, both on earth and standing before God's final judgment throne. Our only responsibility from now until then is to follow Jesus, our "merciful and faithful high priest" (Heb. 2:17). To go where He goes, do what He does, and love who He loves. In so doing, **God's mercy will flow to us and through us**, once again demonstrating that:

The master forgave a huge debt—equivalent to about $3 billion!—which the unforgiving servant could never repay.

The servant refused to forgive his fellow servant's very small debt—equivalent to about $5,000.

The master was upset that the unforgiving servant was not changed by his merciful forgiveness. Instead, the servant was actually misrepresenting the master, even tarnishing the master's reputation, by treating others with such cruelty.

> **Nothing we've done**
> *or will ever do*
> **will make God stop loving us …**
> because of His mercy.

For Bible Nerds (like us) Who Want to Know

In the worship practice of the Old Testament Israelites, the high priest is the one who entered the presence of God in the temple to represent the repentance of God's people and to make an atoning sacrifice for their sins. But as the ultimate high priest, Jesus's representation of humanity before God is perfect.

"For it was indeed fitting that we should have such a high priest, holy, innocent, unstained, separated from sinners, and exalted above the heavens. He has no need, like those high priests, to offer sacrifices daily, first for his own sins and then for those of the people, since he did this once for all when he offered up himself" (Heb. 7:26–27).

Jesus had no sins of His own that needed merciful forgiveness, and He did not need anyone to represent Him to God. In fact, Jesus is not only our high priest, He is also the perfect, once-for-all sacrifice and payment for our sins (Heb. 9:24–28).

"But you, O Lord, are a God merciful and gracious, slow to anger and **abounding in steadfast love** and faithfulness."
Psalm 86:15

"But God shows his love for us in that **while we were still sinners**, Christ died for us."
Romans 5:8

"For I am sure that neither death nor life, nor angels nor rulers, nor things present nor things to come, nor powers, nor height nor depth, nor anything else in all creation, **will be able to separate us from the love of God in Christ Jesus our Lord**."
Romans 8:38–39

"The Lord is not slow to fulfill his promise as some count slowness, **but is patient toward you**, not wishing that any should perish, but that all should reach repentance."
2 Peter 3:9

God's presence goes before us and behind us and beside us ... because of His mercy.

"It is the LORD who goes before you. He will be with you; he
will not leave you or forsake you. Do not fear or be dismayed."
Deuteronomy 31:8

"The LORD is my shepherd; I shall not want. He makes me
lie down in green pastures. He leads me beside still waters.
He restores my soul. He leads me in paths of righteousness for
his name's sake. Even though I walk through the valley of the
shadow of death, I will fear no evil, for you are with me;
your rod and your staff, they comfort me."
Psalm 23:1–4

"And behold, I am with you always, to the end of the age."
Matthew 28:20

"And I will ask the Father, and he will give you
another Helper, to be with you forever, even the Spirit
of truth, whom the world cannot receive, because
it neither sees him nor knows him. You know him,
for he dwells with you and will be in you."
John 14:16–17

**We get to participate in
kingdom acts of mercy …**
because of His mercy.

"A new commandment I give to you, that you love one another: just as I have loved you, you also are to love one another. **By this all people will know that you are my disciples,** if you have love for one another."

John 13:34–35

"**Put on then, as God's chosen ones,** holy and beloved, compassionate hearts, kindness, humility, meekness, and patience, bearing with one another and, if one has a complaint against another, forgiving each other; as the Lord has forgiven you, so you also must forgive. And above all these put on love, which binds everything together in perfect harmony. And let the peace of Christ rule in your hearts, to which indeed you were called in one body. And be thankful. Let the word of Christ dwell in you richly, teaching and admonishing one another in all wisdom, singing psalms and hymns and spiritual songs, with thankfulness in your hearts to God. And whatever you do, in word or deed, do everything in the name of the Lord Jesus, giving thanks to God the Father through him."

Colossians 3:12–17

"Above all, keep loving one another earnestly, since **love covers a multitude of sins.**"

1 Peter 4:8

"But you, beloved, building yourselves up in your most holy faith and praying in the Holy Spirit, keep yourselves in the love of God, waiting for the mercy of our Lord Jesus Christ that leads to eternal life. **And have mercy on those who doubt; save**

others by snatching them out of the fire; to others show
mercy with fear, hating even the garment stained by the flesh."

Jude 20–23

**We are being remade
into the image of Christ ...**
because of His mercy.

"And we all, with unveiled face, beholding the glory of the Lord,
are being transformed into the same image from one
degree of glory to another. For this comes from the Lord who is the Spirit."

2 Corinthians 3:18

"Therefore, if anyone is in Christ, he is a new creation.
The old has passed away; behold, the new has come."

2 Corinthians 5:17

"I have been crucified with Christ. It is no longer I who live,
but Christ who lives in me. And the life I now live in the flesh
I live by faith in the Son of God, who loved me and gave himself for me."

Galatians 2:20

"Beloved, we are God's children now, and what we will be has
not yet appeared; but we know that when he appears
we shall be like him, because we shall see him as he is."

1 John 3:2

Your Turn

5. In light of the preceding verses, describe God's favor toward those who are merciful.

6. Read James 2:12–13. How are these verses both a warning and a promise?

7. Read 1 Peter 1:3–5 below and underline all the ways God has been and continues to be merciful toward you:

> "Blessed be the God and Father of our Lord Jesus Christ!
> According to his great mercy, he has caused us to be
> born again to a living hope through the resurrection
> of Jesus Christ from the dead, to an inheritance that is
> imperishable, undefiled, and unfading, kept in heaven for
> you, who by God's power are being guarded through faith
> for a salvation ready to be revealed in the last time."

8. God's mercy is not earned by our merciful behavior. Rather, we experience His mercy *and then we respond* by extending mercy to others. In this very moment, to whom and how is the Holy Spirit leading you to show mercy?

EXT. JORDAN RIVER

(Simon Z and Jesus walk along the banks of the Jordan.)

SIMON Z: Why Jesse? Why my brother, out of everyone?

JESUS: The man suffered unspeakably for thirty-eight years. It's a long time. And how else could I get your attention?

SIMON Z: My attention?

JESUS *(pauses)*: Your order trained you to be fearless, no?

SIMON Z: No lord but God, to the death.

JESUS: What I did with your brother isn't the last of the trouble I intend to cause.

(Z is into this.)

SIMON Z: You are Messiah, aren't You?

JESUS: Yes.

SIMON Z *(bowing)*: Then I will do anything You ask.

JESUS: I ask you to understand the nature of My mission, Simon.

(Simon is speechless. And confused.)

SIMON Z: Yes. How?

JESUS: Mmm. How, indeed. It's not so easy with distracted humans.

SIMON Z: I have trained for years for this, I am ready to execute Your mission today.

JESUS: We'll see. Show me your weapon.

(Simon Z reverentially removes his beloved sica and its sheath from his belt and hands it to Jesus.)

JESUS: Impressive. That is something.

(Jesus pauses, then throws the knife and sheath into the river. Simon Z's eyes bug out of his head.)

JESUS (CONT'D): You didn't see that coming.

SIMON Z *(Simon's mind races. World upside down—again.)*: You have no use for that?

JESUS: I have a better sword … you'll see. We have much to discuss, just be patient. You've had quite a week.

SIMON Z: Without my sica dagger, why do You need someone like me?

JESUS: I have everything I need. But I WANTED you.

SIMON Z: But why?

JESUS: You are not alone in misunderstanding. But not to worry. I'm preparing something to share with the world. For now, wanting you by My side will have to be enough. No one buys their way into our group because of special skills, Simon.

SIMON Z *(a beat)*: Rabbi?

JESUS: Yes, Simon.

SIMON Z: After what You did at the pool during a high holy feast day, there may be some who might try to … stop You. Even some from my former order, especially if they find out You have a different mission.

JESUS: And what are you going to do, stop them?

SIMON Z: Well, I would be a lot more likely to if You hadn't thrown my sica dagger in the river.

(Jesus laughs. Then turns reflective—)

JESUS: Well, if that day comes … I guess we'll find out.

Prayer Focus

Thank God for the undeserved mercy He has shown you by having His sinless Son die in *your* place for *your* sins. Thank Him for the expectation of His full mercy in the future when Jesus returns. Repent for the ways you've withheld mercy from others, and ask the Lord to empower you by His Holy Spirit to be generous in mercy as an expression of how much He has done for you.

Sample Prayer

Dear God,

I acknowledge that You have not treated me as my sins deserve. Rather, You have mercifully provided Jesus as the willing sacrifice to take the punishment I deserve. I cannot earn Your forgiveness. Jesus, thank You for paying my debt with Your life. Your resurrection assures me of Your power over sin and death, and I look forward to Your return when Your full mercy will be expressed for eternity.

Meanwhile, Lord, as I struggle to live for You on this side of eternity, empower me by Your Holy Spirit to be merciful toward others as You would have me to be.

Amen.

Mary Magdalene

With so many women named Mary in the Bible, this one was distinguished by her hometown of Magdala—one of several fishing villages on the Sea of Galilee. What we know of her from the New Testament is that prior to meeting Jesus, she was a tormented woman, possessed by seven demons. Jesus drove them out, and Mary of Magdala became one of His devoted followers. Her alias in *The Chosen* is "Lilith," and derives from an ancient Middle Eastern term for "female demons" or "wind spirits."

In a culture that tended to view women as being less valuable than men, Mary conversely turned out to be a noteworthy follower of Jesus in that (1) she was among the female disciples who traveled with Him and financially supported His ministry (Luke 8:1–3), (2) she was present at Jesus's crucifixion and burial (Matt. 27:56, 61), and (3) she was the first to witness the empty tomb (John 20:1) and to meet the resurrected Jesus (John 20:11–18; Matt. 28:1; Mark 16:1–6).

Lesson 6

THE PURE IN HEART
and sights unseen

"Blessed are the pure in heart, for they shall see God."

Matthew 5:8

EXT. JERICHO STREET

(Matthew and Simon walk down the street from The Nomad. Simon looks exasperated, shell-shocked. Matthew plots—)

MATTHEW: She can't have gone too far. We'll cover more ground if we split—

SIMON: We're not doing that.

MATTHEW: We can meet at the stables!

SIMON: Didn't you learn anything in there? Mary can obviously take care of herself. YOU can't.

MATTHEW: What if you were cut off from Jesus by something in your past? Wouldn't you want help getting back to Him as soon as possible?

SIMON *(the notion hits Simon like a 2 x 4)*: Okay. We split up. *(pointing—)* North. East. South. West. I'll go north—

MARY MAGDALENE *(off-screen)*: Boys?

(They freeze and turn. ANGLE ON—Mary twenty feet away. She sits on a bench. Drunk. Swaying as she tries to squint the two Matthews and two Simons out of her eyes.)

MATTHEW *(rushing to her)*: Mary!

MARY MAGDALENE: I thought I was dreaming you.

(She trails off, overcome with emotion. Her eyes well. Matthew's look is one of full acceptance. Simon scans the street for signs of danger.)

SIMON: Can you walk?

MARY MAGDALENE: I'm not going anywhere.

MATTHEW: We have to go back.

MARY MAGDALENE: No, I can't.

SIMON: C'mon, Mary. He told us to come for you.

MARY MAGDALENE: No. He already fixed me once and I broke again. I can't face Him.

(As Mary weeps, Simon gives Matthew a look—he's out of ideas. But Matthew kneels before Mary.)

MATTHEW: I'm a bad person, Mary.

MARY MAGDALENE: Matthew …

MATTHEW: No—my whole life, all for me. No faith.

MARY MAGDALENE: I do have faith in Him. Just not in me.

MATTHEW: I'm learning more about Torah and God because of you. I'm studying harder because you are such a great student.

(Matthew prods Simon with a look. Say something!)

SIMON: Remember when we were at Zebedee's? And they lowered that man after breaking Zeb's roof? We did that together. And they got to meet Jesus because of your care for them and your good ideas.

MATTHEW: Ramah is beginning to read and write because of you. He saved you to do all these things.

(Mary breaks down, keels over onto her knees, and vomits the poison she's consumed in the past forty-eight hours. Matthew immediately tends to her, holding back her hair as she coughs and retches.)

MATTHEW (CONT'D): It's all right … it's all right.

The Way It Is

The Old Testament Israelites long understood that anyone who looked directly at God would immediately die. Aware of his own sin and faithlessness, even the prophet Isaiah was afraid when he described meeting God in a vision: "Woe is me! For I am lost; for I am a man of unclean lips, and I dwell in the midst of a people of unclean lips; for my eyes have seen the King, the LORD of hosts!" (Isa. 6:5).

Strange, right? Death-by-holiness is a concept we in the twenty-first century have a hard time wrapping our minds around. But God *is* holy, which means He's without sin. More than that, He's so separate from sin that He can't be near it. He's completely *other*—wholly transcendent above the world He made. So when we disobey His rules—i.e., when we sin—we separate ourselves from the Holy One who loves us, destroying our relationship beyond what we could ever hope to repair. Which is exactly why Jesus became the propitiation for our sin (Rom. 3:25; Heb. 2:17; 1 John 2:2; 4:10). He came to restore our right relationship with God.

There's that big Bible word again ... "propitiation." See page 87 if you already forgot what it means. ☺

Fast-forward to present day where the majority of the population believes they're "good" already. Of course, we tend to define our own goodness by comparing ourselves to the people we deem *not* good, thereby preserving our self-perceived good name and ensuring our good standing before other good people. **But other people aren't the standard of goodness; God is** (Mark 10:18; Luke 18:19). When we compare ourselves to them, we're actually excusing our sins and labeling Scripture we don't like as inapplicable or obsolete. And all the while we're moving further away from the truth: we should be lying prostrate before the

Prostrate: lying facedown on the ground.

For Bible Nerds (like us) Who Want to Know

Just after their extraordinary and miraculous rescue from Egypt through the middle of the Red Sea, Moses was recalling the Israelites' fear about seeing God face to face at Mount Sinai (a.k.a., Horeb) when the Ten Commandments were delivered to them. Out of fear of death, they had insisted Moses represent them before God (Ex. 20:18–21; Deut. 5:1–5). Interestingly, in his reflective remarks, Moses spoke of a greater representative yet to come. #Jesus

Holy God of the Universe, repenting of our sins and praising Him for not striking us dead on arrival.

It's *those* people—the ones who know how not good they really are—that Jesus referred to in the SOM as the "pure in heart."

Oh the irony.

Your Turn

Insecurity and pride are two sides of the same coin because both are the result of self-focus. When we base our identity on Christ, we simultaneously understand our own wretchedness/need for a Savior as well as our preciousness to God, since He sent Jesus to save us.

"But God shows his love for us in that while we were still sinners, Christ died for us."
Romans 5:8

Sabbath:
the weekly practice of abstaining from work in order to rest and to turn one's attention to God and His provision.

1. When it comes to being "good," how do you see yourself? What is your self-perception based on?

The Way It Ought to Be

"Again [Jesus] entered the synagogue, and a man was there with a withered hand. And they watched Jesus, to see whether he would heal him on the Sabbath, so that they might accuse him. And he said to the man with the withered hand, 'Come here.' And he said to them, 'Is it lawful on the Sabbath to do good or to do harm, to save life or to kill?' But they were silent. And he looked around at them with anger, **grieved at their hardness of heart,** and said to the man, 'Stretch out your hand.' He stretched it out, and his hand was restored. The Pharisees

went out and immediately held counsel with the
Herodians against him, how to destroy him."

Mark 3:1–6

A person's heart would have to be pretty hard to be angry
at Jesus for healing on a Saturday instead of a Monday. But
the Pharisees were focused on the letter of their laws instead
of the purposes of God's law. While
God did indeed command Old
Testament Israel to keep certain
religious ceremonies and customs,
those observances were never meant
to be mere matters of outward
behavior. Rather, they were intended
to represent the condition of
the hearts of His people. They were meant to be an
outpouring of what was already inside, because purity of heart
is not measured by man-made rules, nor is it measured by our
own (nonexistent) sinlessness.

The Jews observed the
Sabbath from Friday
night to Saturday
night. New Testament
Christians now practice
the Sabbath on Sunday,
the day Jesus rose
from the dead.

Thank the Lord.

Unfortunately, like the Pharisees, we tend to focus on
outward behavior while giving inward ugliness a pass. We may
not be guilty of "biggie" sins like murder, but we're all guilty of
violating God's perfect and holy law in some capacity. Indeed,
the New Testament teaches that being guilty of one part of
God's law makes us guilty of violating the whole thing: "For
whoever keeps the whole law but fails in one point has become
guilty of all of it" (James 2:10). Bottom line, each one of us has

For Bible Nerds (like us) Who Want to Know

Scripture has a lot to say about "hard-heartedness." Pharaoh and the Egyptians had hearts that were "hardened" against God (Ex. 7–14; 1 Sam. 6:6), as did other enemy nations (Deut. 2:30; Josh. 11:20). The Israelites and some of their leaders were described as having "hardened his heart against turning to the LORD" (2 Chron. 36:13; Ezek. 3:7; Zech. 7:12).

The Gospel of Mark utilizes the same theme (Mark 3:5; 6:52; 8:17; 10:5; 16:14), and three times the book of Hebrews calls readers to heed the warning of Psalm 95:8, "Do not harden your hearts" (Heb. 3:8, 15; 4:7).

In Romans 2, Paul addressed judgmental and hypocritical hard-heartedness and warned, "But because of your hard and impenitent heart you are storing up wrath for yourself on the day of wrath when God's righteous judgment will be revealed" (v. 5).

sin in our lives no matter how much we love Jesus. Recognizing and grieving the sin that separates us from God *and then repenting of it* makes us less like the hypocritical Pharisees and more like the purehearted Mary.

As it turns out, those who've been forgiven much also love much (Luke 7:47). Mary Magdalene may not have been impressive by the world's standards—the people of her day certainly didn't honor her in any way—but her understanding of her own spiritual poverty led to her decision to follow Jesus for the rest of her life. She knew He was the way, the truth, and the life (John 14:6), and she knew that all other roads would lead her back to darkness. She was pure of heart, not because of anything she did or didn't do, and not because she was perfect—she most certainly wasn't. But according to biblical standards, Mary was pure in heart because she surrendered herself to Jesus. And then *He* cleansed her heart, kept her on the narrow road, and led her all the way to heaven, where she was actually *made* perfect, like her Savior.

Oh, that we'd be like Mary, fully understanding that apart from Jesus we're helpless, hopeless, and bound for destruction, but **with Him we're the opposite**. With Him we're helped, hope-filled, and heaven-bound, where instead of being vaporized on sight, we'll see things our minds can't even dream up.

Even more good news?

The seeing starts now.

"None is righteous, no, not one."
Romans 3:10

"For all have sinned and fall short of the glory of God."
Romans 3:23

"If we say we have fellowship with him while we walk in darkness, we lie and do not practice the truth. But if we walk in the light, as he is in the light, we have fellowship with one another, and the blood of Jesus his Son cleanses us from all sin. If we say we have no sin, we deceive ourselves, and the truth is not in us. If we confess our sins, he is faithful and just to forgive us our sins and to cleanse us from all unrighteousness. If we say we have not sinned, we make him a liar, and his word is not in us."
1 John 1:6–10

Repent:
to feel or express sincere regret or remorse about one's wrongdoing; to turn away from sin.

"But, as it is written, 'What no eye has seen, nor ear heard, nor the heart of man imagined, what God has prepared for those who love him.'"
1 Corinthians 2:9

Your Turn

2. In what ways are you like the Pharisees? In what ways are you like Mary?

3. What outward behaviors do you tend to focus on the most, whether your own or someone else's?

4. What attitudes of the heart do you tend to ignore or deprioritize?

Seeing Clearly

"[May] the God of our Lord Jesus Christ, the
Father of glory … give you the Spirit of wisdom
and of revelation in the knowledge of him, <u>having
the eyes of your hearts enlightened</u>, that you may
know what is the hope to which he has called you,
what are the riches of his glorious inheritance in the

For Bible Nerds (like us) Who Want to Know

Someone with true inner moral purity is not just a person of good intentions, but is also sincere, not living a duplicitous lifestyle. The pure in heart are the same in public as they are in private—i.e., they're not hypocrites!

The prophet Jeremiah expressed God's disappointment with the nation of Israel's religious conformity <u>without any change of heart</u>—they were going through the motions. Specifically, they were being circumcised as a sign of their covenant relationship with God, but day to day they weren't much different than the enemies of God. "Behold, the days are coming, declares the LORD, when I will punish all those who are circumcised merely in the flesh … for all these nations are uncircumcised, and all the house of Israel are <u>uncircumcised in heart</u>" (Jer. 9:25–26; see also 4:4; Deut. 10:16; 30:6–8).

"Single-minded" living is, in fact, a theme throughout the SOM wherein Jesus warned His followers, "Beware of practicing your righteousness before other people in order to be seen by them, for then you will have no reward from your Father who is in heaven" (Matt. 6:1). Purity of heart includes quiet acts of kindness (6:2–4), how one prays (6:5–15), religious practices like fasting (6:16–18), what one treasures (6:19–21), and what one focuses on (6:22–24).

saints, and what is the immeasurable greatness of his power toward
us who believe, according to the working of his great might."
Ephesians 1:17–19

If we're not careful, the blessed statements in the SOM can become Sunday school white noise—statements that sound good and Christiany but hold little meaning for us because we're not really paying attention. In actuality, nothing on God's green earth should be more exciting, more awe-inspiring, more hit-the-deck-inducing than the promise that *the pure in heart will see God*. That those who repent and surrender can know Him and ascend His holy hill and enter into His presence **and actually belong there** because He has made it possible (Ps. 24:3–4).

Those of us who follow Jesus will literally see Him face to face in heaven, and the knowledge of that should change everything—because what a day that will be! But we don't even have to wait that long because **God's favor is already upon us.** So while we haven't yet seen Him with our actual eyeballs, the eyes of our hearts have indeed been enlightened. The scales have fallen away (Acts 9:18), and everything we experience going forward now filters through *the hope to which we've been called*, demonstrating again and again God's great love toward those who believe in so many wonderful ways:

"Have you believed because you have seen me? Blessed are those who have not seen and yet have believed."
John 20:29

That's us. ☺

We can see God in His creation.

"The heavens declare the glory of God, and **the sky above proclaims his handiwork.** Day to day pours out speech, and night to night reveals knowledge."

Psalm 19:1–2

"But ask the beasts, and they will teach you; the birds of the heavens, and they will tell you; or the bushes of the earth, and they will teach you; and the fish of the sea will declare to you. Who among all these does not know that the hand of the LORD has done this? **In his hand is the life of every living thing and the breath of all mankind.**"

Job 12:7–10

"In the beginning was the Word, and the Word was with God, and the Word was God. He was in the beginning with God. **All things were made through him,** and without him was not any thing made that was made."

John 1:1–3

"For his invisible attributes, namely, his eternal power and divine nature, **have been clearly perceived**, ever since the creation of the world, in the things that have been made."

Romans 1:20

"For by him all things were created, in heaven and on earth, visible and invisible, whether thrones or dominions or rulers or authorities— **all things were created through him and for him.**"

Colossians 1:16

We can see God in His Church.

"For where two or three are gathered in my name, there am I among them."
Matthew 18:20

We are all made in the image of God (Gen. 1:27), which means our different and varying gifts reflect His MANY gifts. We see God's countless and beautiful attributes in His children and in the collective whole of His Church.

"For as in one body we have many members, and the members do not all have the same function, so we, though many, are one body in Christ, and individually members one of another. Having gifts that differ according to the grace given to us, let us use them: if prophecy, in proportion to our faith; if service, in our serving; the one who teaches, in his teaching; the one who exhorts, in his exhortation; the one who contributes, in generosity; the one who leads, with zeal; the one who does acts of mercy, with cheerfulness."
Romans 12:4–8

"So then you are no longer strangers and aliens, but you are fellow citizens with the saints and members of the household of God, built on the foundation of the apostles and prophets, Christ Jesus himself being the cornerstone, in whom the whole structure, being joined together, grows into a holy temple in the Lord. In him you also are being built together into a dwelling place for God by the Spirit."
Ephesians 2:19–22

"But you are a chosen race, a royal priesthood, a holy nation, a people for his own possession, that you may proclaim the excellencies of him who called you out of darkness into his marvelous light. Once you were not a people, but now you are God's people; once you had not received mercy, but now you have received mercy."

1 Peter 2:9–10

We can see God in the stillness.

"The LORD will fight for you, and you have only to be silent."
Exodus 14:14

"The LORD is my shepherd; I shall not want.
He makes me lie down in green pastures. He leads
me beside still waters. He restores my soul."
Psalm 23:1–3

"Be still, and know that I am God. I will be
exalted among the nations, I will be exalted in the earth!"
Psalm 46:10

"Come to me, all who labor and are heavy laden, and I will give you rest. Take my yoke upon you, and learn from me, for I am gentle and lowly in heart, and you will find rest for your souls.
For my yoke is easy, and my burden is light."
Matthew 11:28–30

We can see God on the horizon.

"Let not your hearts be troubled. Believe in God; believe also in me. In my Father's house are many rooms. If it were not so, would I have told you that I go to prepare a place for you? And if I go and prepare a place for you, I will come again and will take you to myself, that where I am you may be also."
John 14:1–3

"See what kind of love the Father has given to us, that we should be called children of God; and so we are. The reason why the world does not know us is that it did not know him. Beloved, we are God's children now, and what we will be has not yet appeared; but we know that when he appears we shall be like him, because we shall see him as he is. And everyone who thus hopes in him purifies himself as he is pure."
1 John 3:1–3

"Then I saw a new heaven and a new earth, for the first heaven and the first earth had passed away, and the sea was no more. And I saw the holy city, new Jerusalem, coming down out of heaven from God, prepared as a bride adorned for her husband. And I heard a loud voice from the throne saying, 'Behold, the dwelling place of God is with man. He will dwell with them, and they will be his people, and God himself will be with them as their God. He will wipe away every tear from their eyes, and death shall be no more, neither shall there be mourning, nor crying, nor pain anymore, for the former things have passed away.'"

Revelation 21:1–4

Your Turn

5. In light of the preceding verses, describe God's favor toward the pure in heart.

6. In what ways have you clearly seen God in your life or in the lives of those around you?

7. Those who place their faith in Jesus become God's children (John 1:12). How should being a child of God change the way you see and interact with the world around you? Get specific about your circumstances and your people, because seeing God clearly *should* actually change everything.

Placing your faith in Jesus means to repent of your sin and surrender control of your life to Him.

8. Reread John 14:1–3, 1 John 3:1–3, and Revelation 21:1–4 (see pages 112–13), and make a list of the incredible things awaiting the pure in heart.

INT. JESUS'S TENT

(Jesus sits with His back to the entrance, head in His hands, grieving deeply. Not just about John the Baptist's arrest, but about everything He knows somewhere deep in His human-God bone marrow must now be accelerated. Mary Mother pulls open the flap and Mary Magdalene enters. She stands midway between the entrance and Jesus for a moment. Jesus sniffles.)

JESUS *(pulling Himself out of it)*: It's not you. There's quite a lot going on right now. So … it's good to have you back.

MARY MAGDALENE *(lowering her head, tears)*: I don't know what to say.

JESUS: I don't require much.

MARY MAGDALENE: I'm so ashamed. You redeemed me, and I just threw it all away.

JESUS: Well, that's not much of a redemption if it can be lost in a day, is it?

MARY MAGDALENE: I owe You everything, and I just don't think I can do it.

JESUS: Do what?

MARY MAGDALENE: Live up to it. Repay You. How could I leave, how could I go back to the place I was, and I didn't even come back on my own; they had to get me. I just can't live up to it.

JESUS: Well, that's true.

(Mary cries harder.)

JESUS (CONT'D): But you don't have to. I just want your heart. The Father just wants your heart. Give us that, which you already have, and the rest will come in time. Did you really think you'd never struggle or sin again? I know how painful that moment was for you.

MARY MAGDALENE: I shouldn't.

JESUS: Someday. But not here.

MARY MAGDALENE: I'm just so sorry.

JESUS: Look up.

MARY MAGDALENE: I can't.

JESUS: You can. Look at Me. *(She looks up.)* I forgive you. It's over.

Prayer Focus

Talk to God about the condition of your heart. If your loyalty has been divided, if you've continued living for yourself, if you've judged yourself by a standard other than Jesus's—admit those things to the Lord. Acknowledge your inability to live a sinless life. Ask Him to forgive you and to make your heart pure.

Thank God that salvation depends on the purity of Jesus's life and His sacrificial death. Ask Him to empower you by His Holy Spirit to live out of gratitude in the purity of heart that Jesus provides. Ask Him to help you recognize His work in and around you now as you anticipate someday seeing Him face to face.

Sample Prayer

Dear God,

As much as I might try to look good to other people, I acknowledge that I sinfully fall short of Your standard of goodness. Please forgive me for the impurity of my sin and for the hypocritical ways in which I've tried to cover it. Forgive me for trying to feel better about my own sinfulness by condemning those around me. Thank You for providing salvation through faith in Jesus rather than through my inadequate efforts.

Please purify my heart and empower me by Your Spirit to recognize Your work in and around me, and to live joyfully for You now until I meet You face to face in eternity.

Amen.

Andrew, Brother of Simon Peter

Growing up in Bethsaida on the Sea of Galilee as brother of Simon Peter, Andrew was involved in the family's fishing business (Matt. 4:18–20; Mark 1:16–17). He'd been a disciple of John the Baptist before deciding to follow Jesus (John 1:35–40), and he is credited with quickly recruiting his brother Simon Peter to follow as well (vv. 41–42). At some point, Andrew and Simon Peter relocated to nearby Capernaum on the Sea of Galilee, which became the headquarters for Jesus's ministry (Mark 1:29; 2:1). Andrew appears to have been a positive, can-do kind of guy who made himself and his resources available to Jesus (like the fish and loaves at the feeding of the five thousand in John 6:8–9) and who was very approachable (John 12:20–22).

Andrew is mentioned once in Acts, and ancient tradition reports that his ministry after Acts was in places like Achaia (Greece), Anatolia (a region of modern Turkey), and Macedonia, with a trip to Scythia (a region of modern Ukraine and Russia), where God utilized him to rescue Matthias from cannibals. Hippolytus reported that Andrew was crucified on an olive tree at Patras, a town in Achaia (ca. AD 70). Tradition suggests it was an X-shaped cross (a "saltire"). Andrew's bones are thought to have been relocated in the fourth century to Scotland, and the eighth-century King Hungus of the Picts is said to have won a promised victory in battle under a saltire symbol in the sky. Thus, Andrew has been the patron saint of Scotland ever since.

Lesson 7

THE PEACEMAKERS
and what they pursue

"Blessed are the peacemakers, for they shall be called sons [and daughters] of God."

Matthew 5:9

EXT. SEA OF GALILEE (DAY)

(The brothers fish.)

SIMON: Like old times, huh?

ANDREW: As you said, no one ever has to guess what's going on in your head.

SIMON: There's nothing in my head. This? It's in our bones … don't have to think.

ANDREW: Must be nice, having nothing in your head.

SIMON: Don't be smart, it's just a saying.

ANDREW: That was true when you plucked the head of grain at Wadi Kelt.

SIMON: Everybody did that! Except … Mary.

ANDREW: She'd already done her part.

SIMON: You think you're never gonna make another mistake in your life?

ANDREW: She was gone for days!

SIMON: Two. Don't exaggerate.

ANDREW: Me not to exagg—are you telling me not to exaggerate? That's—WOW.

SIMON: Look—she went through something horrible and terrifying, and she dealt with it the best way she knew how.

ANDREW: She should've gone to Jesus.

SIMON: She knows that now! If you remember, Jesus was disarming crazy Simon of his dagger.

ANDREW: Oh *he's* the crazy Simon?

SIMON *(shrugs)*: I'm a married man who worked an honest trade.

ANDREW: Worked an honest trade dishonestly!

SIMON: It's how I met Jesus. Unexpected roads …

ANDREW: Gambling? Brawling? That also unexpected?

SIMON: You gambled too!

ANDREW: And I'll never do it again! And if I'm ever tempted, I'll ask the Rabbi for help. Certainly won't do anything selfish … leave the group stranded at camp for two days starving, or put Jesus on edge, make Him snap at the Pharisees who are hunting us down now!

SIMON: He was grieving John's arrest, and they're not hunting us down! You're so dramatic—

ANDREW: Word reaches Jerusalem that He claimed the title Son of Man and Lord of the Sabbath, they'll hunt Him down, they'll put Him away, it could completely ruin all the plans for the sermon, erase all the momentum we've gained! *That's* what I'm afraid of!

SIMON: Jerusalem doesn't even open the mail from Wadi Kelt. Andrew—this is just fear talking.

ANDREW: I've been at this longer than you. When they decide they don't like you, it's over. John! John might spend his life in prison.

SIMON: Herod arrested John, not the Sanhedrin.

ANDREW: Sanhedrin arrest people all the time!

SIMON: You're the one who told me He was the Messiah. Am I gonna have to be the one to remind you now?

ANDREW: The very fact that He's the Messiah means there's going to be trouble. You get it? Maybe even a war.

SIMON: If you were building an army, would you start with Little James and Thaddaeus?

ANDREW: Simon—

SIMON: You think He's drawing up military plans every time He goes away to desolate places?

ANDREW: He never comes back with anything!

SIMON: You know what? Let's just fish, all right? Can we?

(They sit back and wait on their respective sides. Andrew staring west, Simon staring east, when something off-screen turns him ashen. Simon sees Roman troops in the distance, marching along the eastern shore. They move toward where Jesus is teaching up on the knoll. No one from camp notices the soldiers yet, still far off. Simon remains extremely calm.)

SIMON: Andrew? My little brother whom I love very much?

ANDREW: What?

SIMON: I need you to take a very long, deep breath. Can you do that?

ANDREW: What? Why?

SIMON: Just please. Ask God to give you peace before—

(Andrew instinctively follows Simon's eyes. He turns around, ignoring all the instructions. As he lurches up in panic, Simon exhales and closes his eyes … why did he even bother?)

The Road Less Traveled

There are typically two approaches to peacemaking, neither of which offers much in the way of actual peace. The first is called "peace*faking*," wherein a person seeks to avoid conflict by pretending like there isn't any. They smile and say they're fine while they sweep the things they'd rather not deal with under the nearest rug. Incidentally, swept things don't go away—they lie in wait. The second is called "peace*breaking*," wherein a person seeks to resolve conflict by demanding it be acknowledged and dealt with. Like, NOW.

As different as the two approaches seem, they have similar origins:

SELF-protection, SELF-righteousness, and SELF-entitlement—just to name a few. Are you sensing a theme?

General twenty-first-century wisdom actually teaches that in order to be happy, we must first please *ourselves*, which basically means whatever we think, feel, or want takes precedence over everything and everyone else. But the steady decline in our collective mental health, along with the rise of things like mass shootings, substance abuse, divorce, and suicide, proves that what the culture has been preaching to us isn't working. Because while our focus is on SELF, in the seventh blessing of the SOM, Jesus's focus was on peacemaking.

And He gave HimSELF to do it.

Your Turn

1. To what extent are you a peace*faker* and/or a peace*breaker*, and why?

The Way of Peace

"Lifting up his eyes, then, and seeing that a large crowd was coming toward him, Jesus said to Philip, 'Where are we to buy bread, so that these people may eat?' He said this to test him, for he himself knew what he would do. Philip answered him, 'Two hundred denarii worth of bread would not be enough for each of them to get a little.' One of his disciples, Andrew, Simon Peter's brother, said to him, 'There is a boy here who has five barley loaves and two fish, but what are they for so many?' Jesus said, 'Have the people sit down.' Now there was much grass in the place. So the men sat down, about five thousand in number. Jesus then took the loaves, and when he had given thanks, he distributed them to those who were seated. So also the fish, as much as they wanted. And when they had eaten their fill, he told his disciples, 'Gather up the leftover fragments, that nothing may be lost.' So they gathered them up and filled twelve baskets with fragments from the five barley loaves left by those who had eaten."

John 6:5–13

Seems like Andrew was pretty good at following Jesus. He was eager and earnest and easy. He brought his questions and confusion to Jesus—along with a little boy's loaves and fish. And it paid off, because Jesus took what Andrew gave Him and turned it into something big that fed a bunch of people and also changed the world. But more on that in a minute because, in spite of the miracles, even a guy like Andrew had to reconcile himself to a new way of doing things. He had to release his preconceived notions of what God was like, who He would choose, and how the kingdom of heaven was going to be established—starting with Jesus's followers.

The disciples were an unconventional lot because Jesus welcomed everyone, which meant Andrew had to figure out how to get along with a Roman-sympathizing tax collector and an

For Bible Nerds (like us) Who Want to Know

In his New Testament letter, without explicitly mentioning the SOM, Jesus's brother James echoed several of the Beatitudes in the short space of a few verses:

"But the wisdom from above is first pure, then peaceable, gentle, open to reason, full of mercy and good fruits, impartial and sincere. And a harvest of righteousness is sown in peace by those who make peace" (James 3:17–18).

In this collection of Beatitude characteristics (i.e., purity, mercy, righteousness, meekness, etc.), James mentioned "peace" three times. In doing so, he used a phrase for "those who make peace" (*poiousin eirēnēn*, v. 18). In the Gospel of Matthew, Jesus used the compound word "peacemakers" (*eirēnopoioi*, Matt. 5:9; Col. 1:20). Thus, both were talking about peace as a goal, as something that God's people aim to "make" (*poieō*). It's important to note here that the subject is not merely being peaceful, but actually being someone who makes peace— someone who invests time and energy in working toward peace as a goal.

anti-Roman zealot, not to mention the large crowds of people that were always hanging around. No doubt he and the rest of the gang had to put aside their own opinions and feelings in order to participate in what Jesus was doing and teaching. And Jesus instructed His followers to make peace—not to fake it or to demand resolution on their terms, but instead to:

a. Be reconciled to one another (Matt. 5:21–26).

b. Be respectful of the opposite gender and remain faithful in marriage (Matt. 5:27–32).

c. Keep their word (Matt. 5:33–37).

d. Avoid retaliation (Matt. 5:38–42).

e. Love their enemies (Matt. 5:43–48).

f. Abstain from trying to impress (Matt. 6:1–8, 16–18).

g. Forgive one another (Matt. 6:9–15).

In other words, peacemaking is really, really hard! Nevertheless, **the degree to which we make peace with one another reflects the degree to which we trust our Leader**, because He tells us to make peace and because making peace almost always requires us to give something up—to deny ourselves like Jesus did when He made peace with God on our behalf (Matt. 16:24).

No doubt denying himself and obeying Jesus's teaching were as counterintuitive for Andrew as they are for us. But blessed are the peacemakers, because God's wisdom actually preserves our lives, not to mention our relationships; it keeps us from SELF-*destructing*. Blessed are those who seek peace and pursue it with the very people Jesus died for (#everyone).

"For he himself is our peace, who has made us both one and has broken down in his flesh the dividing wall of hostility by abolishing the law of commandments expressed in ordinances, that he might create in himself one new man in place of the two, so making peace, and might reconcile us both to God in one body through the cross, thereby killing the hostility. And he came and preached peace to you who were far off and peace to those who were near. For through him we both have access in one Spirit to the Father."
Ephesians 2:14–18

"And he said to all, 'If anyone would come after me, let him deny himself and take up his cross daily and follow me. For whoever would save his life will lose it, but whoever loses his life for my sake will save it.'"
Luke 9:23–24

"Turn away from evil and do good; seek peace and pursue it."
Psalm 34:14

And blessed are those who give their wants and needs to the Savior, because in His hands stuff gets multiplied.

Be it loaves and fish or children of the King.

Your Turn

2. Who in your life is difficult to make peace with, and why?

3. Read the passage below from Philippians and underline some of the ways we can choose to make peace, paying particular attention to Christ's example at the end of the passage.

"Do nothing from selfish ambition or conceit, but in humility count others more significant than yourselves. Let each of you look not only to his own interests, but also to the interests of others. Have this mind among yourselves, which is yours in Christ Jesus, who, though he was in the form of God, did not count equality with God a thing to be grasped, but emptied himself, by taking the form of a servant, being born in the likeness of men. And being found in human form, he humbled himself by becoming obedient to the point of death, even death on a cross."

Philippians 2:3–8

For Bible Nerds (like us) Who Want to Know

As any parent of young children can testify, the temptation to make conflict instead of peace is still with us. While adults can be more subtle than children, the temptation to be less than peaceful continues. James specifically confronted his readers about worldly warring in the church, and he used the terms "friendship" and "enemy" to do it.

"What causes quarrels and what causes fights among you? Is It not this, that your passions are at war within you? You desire and do not have, so you murder. You covet and cannot obtain, so you fight and quarrel. You do not have, because you do not ask. You ask and do not receive, because you ask wrongly, to spend it on your passions. You adulterous people! Do you not know that friendship with the world is enmity with God? Therefore whoever wishes to be a friend of the world makes himself an enemy of God" (James 4:1–4).

4. What are some practical ways you can implement these peacemaking tactics today?

Beautiful Feet

"How beautiful upon the mountains are the feet of him who brings
good news, who publishes peace, who brings good news of happiness,
who publishes salvation, who says to Zion, 'Your God reigns.'"

Isaiah 52:7

"The wolf shall dwell with the lamb, and the leopard shall lie down with the young goat, and the calf and the lion and the fattened calf together; and a little child shall lead them. The cow and the bear shall graze; their young shall lie down together; and the lion shall eat straw like the ox. The nursing child shall play over the hole of the cobra, and the weaned child shall put his hand on the adder's den. They shall not hurt or destroy in all my holy mountain; for the earth shall be full of the knowledge of the LORD as the waters cover the sea."
Isaiah 11:6–9

Being at peace with God makes it possible to live in peace with others, because peace is an overflow of what's already inside. When Jesus said that peacemakers would be called sons of God, He wasn't talking about the first moment of salvation, because being a peacemaker isn't how we enter into the family of God—that only happens through faith in Jesus as the One who died for our sins and rose again to new life. No, the Sermon on the Mount isn't about how we begin new life in Jesus; it's about our new identity once we do.

To be called by a particular name is to be identified as having a particular characteristic connecting us to something or someone. And one of God's many characteristics is that He's relentlessly loving, which is why He entered *into* the story. Our Creator and King sacrificed Himself to save us from ourselves and to usher in the eternal kingdom of peace. Once we belong to the kingdom, we're charged with making peace with others too, knowing our heavenly Father—the King—loves the very people we sometimes find ourselves at odds with. We're representing Him to them.

And the knowledge of that should change everything. As God's peacemaking children, we are drawing others to Him, because as Jesus said: "By this all people will know that you are my disciples, if you have love for one another" (John 13:35). Our love—i.e., our decision to live in peace as long as it depends on us (Rom. 12:18)—reflects God's very nature, thereby showing those around us who He is. Which means blessed are the feet of the one who brings the good news of God's love to others, the one who publishes peace, the one who lives out God's kingdom qualities on earth, because not only will others be drawn to heaven as a result, but we will also have the greatest honor of all:

We will be known as children of God …

along with all the perks that come with:

Children of the King are counted as righteous.
Which means you don't have to feel shame about your past,
or defensiveness in the present, or anxiousness about the future.
You can let all that go because God has made the way for peace.

"But now in Christ Jesus you who once were far off have been brought
near by the blood of Christ. For he himself is our peace,
who has made us both one and has broken down in his flesh the
dividing wall of hostility by abolishing the law of commandments
expressed in ordinances, that he might create in himself one new man
in place of the two, so making peace, and might reconcile us both
to God in one body through the cross, thereby killing the hostility.

And he came and preached peace to you who were far off and peace to those who were near. For through him we both have access in one Spirit to the Father."

Ephesians 2:13–18

"And now, little children, abide in him, so that when he appears we may have confidence and not shrink from him in shame at his coming. If you know that he is righteous, you may be sure that everyone who practices righteousness has been born of him."

1 John 2:28–29

"See what kind of love the Father has given to us, that we should be called children of God; and so we are. The reason why the world does not know us is that it did not know him. Beloved, we are God's children now, and what we will be has not yet appeared; but we know that when he appears we shall be like him, because we shall see him as he is. And everyone who thus hopes in him purifies himself as he is pure."

1 John 3:1–3

Children of the King have an inheritance waiting in heaven. You don't need to fight for what's yours. God has already preserved it for you, thereby ensuring your peace.

"Then the King will say to those on his right, 'Come, you who are blessed by my Father, **inherit the kingdom prepared for you from the foundation of the world.**'"

Matthew 25:34

"For you did not receive the spirit of slavery to fall back into fear, but you have received the Spirit of adoption as sons [and daughters], by whom we cry, 'Abba! Father!' The Spirit himself bears witness with our spirit that we are children of God, **and if children, then heirs—heirs of God and fellow heirs with Christ**, provided we suffer with him in order that we may also be glorified with him."

Romans 8:15–17

"Whatever you do, work heartily, as for the Lord and not for men, **knowing that from the Lord you will receive the inheritance as your reward.** You are serving the Lord Christ."

Colossians 3:23–24

"Blessed be the God and Father of our Lord Jesus Christ! According to his great mercy, he has caused us to be born again to a living hope through the resurrection of Jesus Christ from the dead, **to an inheritance that is imperishable, undefiled, and unfading, kept in heaven for you**, who by God's power are being guarded through faith for a salvation ready to be revealed in the last time."

1 Peter 1:3–5

Children of the King
are permanently established.
You never have to feel insecure or unsure or
uncared for. God has firmly established you.
You need only abide in His peace.

"For to us a child is born, to us a son is given; and the government
shall be upon his shoulder, and his name shall be called Wonderful
Counselor, Mighty God, Everlasting Father, Prince of Peace. Of
the increase of his government and of peace there will be no end, on
the throne of David and over his kingdom, to establish it and
to uphold it with justice and with righteousness
from this time forth and forevermore."
Isaiah 9:6–7

"For I know the plans I have for you, declares the LORD, plans for
welfare and not for evil, to give you a future and a hope."
Jeremiah 29:11

"But to all who did receive him, who believed in his name,
he gave the right to become children of God, who were
born, not of blood nor of the will of the flesh
nor of the will of man, but of God."
John 1:12–13

"And we know that for those who love God
all things work together for good, for those
who are called according to his purpose."

Romans 8:28

Your Turn

5. In light of the preceding verses, describe God's favor toward peacemakers.

6. How would shifting focus from yourself to God enable you to live more peaceably with others? Be specific.

7. Reread the verse below and do an honest self-check. By God's grace, who are you loving well? Who do you need to love differently and in what way(s)?

"By this all people will know that you are my
disciples, if you have love for one another."

John 13:35

8. Jesus didn't always "keep the peace." He often found Himself at odds with those who opposed His mission. But there's a difference between extending peace toward others and their refusal to accept peace (Rom. 12:16–18). According to James 1:5, where does wisdom to know the difference come from?

EXT. DISCIPLES' CAMP (DUSK)

(The disciples—everyone except Philip, Andrew, Thaddaeus, and Little James—are scattered about, slowly preparing for bed, clearly dejected. Zee and Simon are on opposite ends, standing guard. Suddenly, Zee's eyes widen as he looks into a clearing outside the camp—

ZEE'S POV—It's Jesus, clearly in intense prayer as He paces.)

ZEE: He's back!

(Everyone reacts quickly. Zee hustles through the clearing toward Jesus.)

ZEE (CONT'D): Teacher! Are You hurt? What happened?

(Jesus stops praying, turns.)

JESUS: Ah, I suppose I should not be surprised YOU would spot me.

(The others arrive in spurts. Mary Mother hugs Jesus.)

JESUS (CONT'D): Hi, *Eema.*

NATHANAEL: Rabbi, are You safe?

SIMON: Did anyone follow You?

JESUS: Yes, I'm safe. And they just wanted to talk.

(Matthew smiles big, a rare sight.)

MATTHEW: I'm very happy.

(Jesus chuckles.)

JESUS: I'm glad, Matthew.

SIMON: Just talk?

JESUS: Quintus wanted to talk, yes, but the Romans, they don't find Me much of a threat, which is fine.

ZEE *(aside)*: Hopefully that'll change soon.

JOHN: So what were You doing out there?

JESUS: Praying, John. Remember, there's a big event to prepare for.

BIG JAMES: Rabbi, with all due respect, You couldn't have told us that You were back first? You were grabbed by Roman soldiers with weapons; we were all worried sick.

JESUS: Did I not tell you that I would be back, and to keep planning? … You all are going to have to learn how to do this regardless of what's happening, good or bad. Things are only going to get more difficult; you can't just shut down when you're fearful. And what are you going to do when I'm no longer here?

JOHN: Yes, we are still figuring this out.

SIMON: Yes, but we can do better—we will do better.

JOHN: Rabbi, Philip said the Baptizer gave his followers a prayer in addition to the daily traditional prayers. Perhaps You could do the same?

BIG JAMES: Yes, I'd like to learn more about what You're saying when You're out alone.

JESUS: Now, now you are behaving like true students, this is what I like to see. And prayer is the first step in getting the mind and the heart right; it's why you see Me go to it so often.

SIMON: So teach us to pray like You do … please.

JESUS: When we pray, we want to be sure to first start with acknowledging our Father in heaven, and His greatness. So you can say, "Our Father in heaven, hallowed be Your name." And we always want to be sure to do God's will, and not our own. So we say, "Your kingdom come, Your will be done, on earth as it is in heaven …"

Prayer Focus

Talk to God about peace and peacemaking, and thank Him for providing it through the life, death, and resurrection of Jesus. Ask Him to help you lean into His peace in your own life. Commit yourself to being an instrument in His hands, and ask Him to give you the necessary wisdom and fortitude to do what He's asking you to do—no matter how others may respond—knowing that ultimately peace is a characteristic of God's children.

Sample Prayer

Dear heavenly Father,

Thank You for creating peace in my life by sending Your Son Jesus to rescue me from sin. I acknowledge that it's a gift from You and that it cost You dearly. I confess I don't always let Your peace rule in my heart, so please help me with that. Help me trust You so much that I'm willing to work toward peace with others—even when it might cost me something. I want to be a tool in Your hands for making peace. So help me recognize the opportunities You provide, and grant me Your Spirit's wisdom and power to work toward peace as Your child.

Amen.

Thaddaeus (a.k.a., Judas, Son of James; a.k.a., Jude)

As with some of the other apostles like Simon Peter and Levi Matthew, Judas Thaddaeus had several names. "Judas" was common in the New Testament era, so it's no surprise that two men among the twelve apostles shared the name. The potential confusion was evident from the beginning, so much so that John literally introduced him as "Judas (not Iscariot)" (John 14:22). Luke called him "Judas the son of James" (Luke 6:16; Acts 1:13), but Matthew and Mark both used his Greek name, "Thaddaeus" (Matt. 10:3; Mark 3:18).

a.k.a., NOT Judas Iscariot who betrayed Jesus

Little is known about Thaddaeus, and we hear him speak only once in the Gospels when he asks Jesus this question: "Lord, how is it that you will manifest yourself to us, and not to the world?" (John 14:22)—perhaps indicating his desire for the salvation message to reach the whole world. Tradition suggests that Thaddaeus ministered in Syria in the city of Edessa, along the Euphrates River, and in Armenia. He is believed to have preached the gospel in the midst of pagan priests and to have taken part in exorcisms.

His name is mentioned multiple times alongside Simon the Zealot (Matt. 10:3–4; Mark 3:18; Luke 6:15–16; Acts 1:13), and some traditions pair the two in ministry in Parthia (modern-day Iran). Stories of their martyrdom together include being clubbed to death and sawn into pieces (ca. AD 72).

Others mentioned in Scripture who were named "Judas":

one of Jesus's brothers, who was also the likely author of the New Testament book of Jude (Matt. 13:55; Mark 6:3)

a Galilean rebel (Acts 5:37)

a man in Damascus (Acts 9:11)

the letter carrier Judas Barsabbas (Acts 15:22–32)

Lesson 8

THE PERSECUTED
and the precious

"Blessed are those who are persecuted for righteousness'

sake, for theirs is the kingdom of heaven."

Matthew 5:10

EXT. CHORAZIN PLATEAU (DAY)

(Little James, Thaddaeus, and Nathanael hike through the foothills.)

NATHANAEL: I think the knoll east of the NahalKur River looks promising.

THADDAEUS: But it's a knoll. He won't be high enough for people to see and hear Him.

LITTLE JAMES: And there are trees to the south that obstruct the view of the Sea of Galilee—which He specifically requested.

NATHANAEL: Why does He need a view of the sea?

THADDAEUS: I think He wanted to be high enough up.

LITTLE JAMES: What about the hills north of Chorazin? There's plenty of height. His voice would carry.

NATHANAEL: It's too steep of a climb.

THADDAEUS: And the distance is too far for the people from Tiberias and Magdala. He said He wanted to keep it within a day's walk from those cities.

LITTLE JAMES: Maybe we're looking too far north.

NATHANAEL: What did He request? A grove of juniper or gum trees on the backside where we could camp the night before?

THADDAEUS: It's like He already knows the place.

NATHANAEL: Yeah, we just have to find it.

(OFF—sheep baaing and goats bleating in the distance. The disciples hike up a small ridge in the direction of the sound. As they crest the ridge, a mount with some trees on the side comes into view. Blocking them is a three-and-a-half-foot-high stone fence, and a vast pasture extends beyond. A haggard wooden sign with Aramaic on it stands in front of the wall.)

THADDAEUS: "No trespassing. Violators will be prosecuted."

(A female goatherd tends her flock while watching the disciples.)

NATHANAEL: Shalom, shalom! We mean no harm, sister.

THADDAEUS: We're here on friendly business.

(She approaches cautiously.)

NATHANAEL: Behind where you are, is that a good view of the Sea of Galilee?

GOATHERD: Go away.

NATHANAEL: That's not very friendly.

THADDAEUS: Excuse me … are you the owner?

GOATHERD: It's closed to visitors!

LITTLE JAMES: It's very important that we speak to him—

(Goatherd is totally uninterested. She wanders out of sight. Little James and Thaddaeus share a knowing look, wry smiles.)

THADDAEUS: This is probably the spot.

NATHANAEL: What? Why? It's completely repellent.

LITTLE JAMES: Exactly.

Square Peg, Round Hole

We all want to feel like we belong. Literally every person on the face of the earth desires to fit in—to be liked, included, and esteemed. We're driven by it, but it can get us into trouble since we tend to look for belonging in all the wrong places (i.e., anywhere on planet earth).

Stick a pin in that.

As we've been studying, there is tremendous blessing in following Jesus. Knowing Him gives life meaning and purpose, joy and hope. But belonging to God's kingdom actually makes us foreigners everywhere else, because **choosing to follow Him means leaving the world behind.** It means hearing, seeing, doing, and evaluating things in a completely new way. And there's the rub, because once we belong to God, we no longer belong here.

Which would be fine but for the fact that we still live here.

"Beloved, I urge you as sojourners and exiles to abstain from the passions of the flesh, which wage war against your soul. Keep your conduct among the Gentiles honorable, so that when they speak against you as evildoers, they may see your good deeds and glorify God on the day of visitation."
1 Peter 2:11–12

Your Turn

1. What and who are competing with your sincere desire to belong to God? In other words, apart from Him, where do you long to fit in, and why?

Not as the World Gives

Anyone can accept Jesus's invitation to follow Him. But just as Thaddaeus's (a.k.a., Judas NOT Iscariot's) question/concern indicated, not everyone will.

"Judas (not Iscariot) said to him, 'Lord, how is it that you will manifest yourself to us, and not to the world?' Jesus answered him, 'If anyone loves me, he will keep my word, and my Father will love him, and we will come to him and make our home with him. Whoever does not love me does not keep my words. And the word that you hear is not mine but the Father's who sent me. These things I have spoken to you while I am still with you. But the Helper, the Holy Spirit, whom the Father will send in my name, he will teach you all things and bring to your remembrance all that I have said to you. Peace I leave with you; my peace I give to you. Not as the world gives do I give to you. Let not your hearts be troubled, neither let them be afraid.'"

John 14:22–27

As indicated in the previous three Beatitudes, those chosen by Jesus are merciful, purehearted, and peacemaking in their interactions with others. But the eighth Beatitude indicates that those efforts won't always be reciprocated by the world. Jesus warned His followers to not expect mercy in return for mercy (Matt. 18:21–35). Or the absence of duplicity in return for pureheartedness (2 Tim. 3:12–13; 1 Pet. 4:1–5). Or peace as a result of their efforts to make peace (Rom. 12:14–18). But despite the somber news, Jesus promised we'd receive something even better: the Holy

Spirit and all the resources that come with Him.

And therein lies the belonging our hearts are truly longing for, because the world is a tough place. Even when we do achieve happiness, it's not permanent; our circumstances are in a constant state of ebb and flow. What's here today is often gone tomorrow, which is why the blessings in the SOM are so encouraging—they're eternal. They don't change or fade like absolutely everything else in our dying world. "Not as the world gives do I give to you" (John 14:27) is a bit of an understatement (no offense, Jesus) because, as we're learning, the favor of God is not only what our hearts truly long for, it's what we're made for. As the saying goes, we were created with a God-shaped hole in our hearts that only He can fill—that the Holy Spirit *does* fill. All other longings are misplaced; God is the One we desire. The problem is that we don't always know it, which is exactly what Judas Thaddaeus was referring to when he asked, "Lord, how is it that you will manifest yourself to us, and not to the world?" (John 14:22).

Why *do* some people believe and others do not? Or more to the SOM point—why will some of us believe and others will want to persecute us for it? To that end, how could there be *blessing* in that?

And now we've arrived at the best part of the whole study.

For Bible Nerds (like us) Who Want to Know

Paul instructed the new churches in the southern Galatian region that "through many tribulations we must enter the kingdom of God" (Acts 14:22).

At first glance, suffering for doing good doesn't make sense. But the persistence of sin in the face of God's goodness and righteousness is a common response, so it shouldn't be a surprise that people also respond rebelliously against righteousness in God's people.

Peter also addressed the issue of being persecuted for righteousness in one of his New Testament letters:

"Now who is there to harm you if you are zealous for what is good? But even if you should suffer for righteousness' sake, you will be blessed. Have no fear of them, nor be troubled, but in your hearts honor Christ the Lord as holy, always being prepared to make a defense to anyone who asks you for a reason for the hope that is in you; yet do it with gentleness and respect, having a good conscience, so that, when you are slandered, those who revile your good behavior in Christ may be put to shame. For it is better to suffer for doing good, if that should be God's will, than for doing evil" (1 Pet. 3:13–17).

Your Turn

2. The Holy Spirit is easy to take for granted, which is perhaps why His presence sometimes seems less exciting to us than the presence of worldly things like money, relationships, accolades, etc. But according to the verses below, what eternal benefits does the Holy Spirit's presence bring about in our earthly lives?

> "Now the Lord is the Spirit, and
> where the Spirit of the Lord is, there
> is freedom. And we all, with unveiled
> face, beholding the glory of the
> Lord, are being transformed into
> the same image from one degree
> of glory to another. For this comes
> from the Lord who is the Spirit."
> 2 Corinthians 3:17–18

3. Read Galatians 5:22–23 and write down the fruits of the Holy Spirit in the blanks following question 4. Why is the produce metaphor significant (i.e., does an apple tree "try really hard" to grow apples)?

4. Notice how the fruits of the Spirit correspond to the blessed statements of Matthew 5. Draw lines connecting the fruits to the corresponding SOM attitudes produced in the followers of Jesus (note: there are no wrong answers here!).

Fruits of the Spirit	Blessed Are	
_____	The poor in spirit	a. God draws us to Himself.
_____	Those who grieve	b. God forgives us and indwells us.
_____	The meek	
_____	Those who hunger and thirst for righteousness	c. God enables us to have SOM attitudes of the heart.
_____	The merciful	d. God pours out His favor on those with SOM attitudes.
_____	The pure in heart	
_____	The peacemakers	In other words, God does all the things.
_____	Those who are persecuted	

Out of the World

"If the world hates you, know that it has hated me before it hated you. <u>If you were of the world, the world would love you as its own; but because you are not of the world, but I chose you out of the world, therefore the world hates you.</u> Remember the word that I said to you: 'A servant is not greater than his master.' If they persecuted me, they will also persecute you."

John 15:18–20

"Blessed are the poor in spirit, for theirs is the kingdom of heaven" (Matt. 5:3).

"Blessed are those who are persecuted for righteousness' sake, for theirs is the kingdom of heaven" (Matt. 5:10).

=

Bookends

The promise in the last Beatitude is an echo of the first—like bookends. Because despite any grief we may suffer this side of eternity on account of Jesus, His followers can anticipate future joy with Him in heaven. Paul phrased it like this, "The Spirit himself bears witness with our spirit that we are children of God, and if children, then heirs—heirs of God and fellow heirs with

Furthermore, the promises of Beatitudes 2–7 are all future tense: "shall." But the bookending promise of Beatitudes 1 and 8 is present tense: "For theirs _is_ the kingdom of heaven."

Christ, provided we suffer with him in order that we may also be glorified with him" (Rom. 8:16–17).

So what's the promise? The Spirit who lives inside us is the constant herald of the very best news—His still, small voice in our ear repeating again and again that we are God's precious children, that this world is not our home, and that our future is in a paradise called heaven. But our joy doesn't merely reside in anticipation of the future. In the bookending Beatitudes, the kingdom of heaven *already is* for those who trust in Jesus. The kingdom of heaven is present on earth in the lives of Jesus's chosen people.

And the knowledge of that changes everything! Because in the midst of our struggles and grief and pain and even persecution for our faith in Jesus, we find His heavenly kingdom is already here—the kingdom we belong to. And while our new reality may indeed be invisible, even nonsensical to those who are perishing (1 Cor. 1:18–31), here's the truth that gives life and sustains life here on earth:

The Lord our God—King of the Universe and of our hearts—reigns ... over all things and all people for all time, including the past, present, and future.

"The LORD will reign forever, your God,

O Zion, to all generations. Praise the LORD!"

Psalm 146:10

"So shall my word be that goes out from my

mouth; it shall not return to me empty, but

it shall accomplish that which I purpose,

and shall succeed in the thing for which I sent it."

Isaiah 55:11

"The saying is trustworthy, for:

If we have died with him, we will also live with him;

if we endure, **we will also reign with him;**

if we deny him, he also will deny us;

if we are faithless, he remains faithful—

for he cannot deny himself."

2 Timothy 2:11–13

"Then the seventh angel blew his trumpet, and there were

loud voices in heaven, saying, 'The kingdom of the world

has become the kingdom of our Lord and of his Christ,

and he shall reign forever and ever.'"

Revelation 11:15

Which means He is our refuge ...

in times of heartache and fear and

need and persecution.

"God is our refuge and strength, a very present help in trouble. Therefore we will not fear though the earth gives way, though the mountains be moved into the heart of the sea, though its waters roar and foam, though the mountains tremble at its swelling. There is a river whose streams make glad the city of God, the holy habitation of the Most High. God is in the midst of her; she shall not be moved; God will help her when morning dawns. The nations rage, the kingdoms totter; he utters his voice, the earth melts. The LORD of hosts is with us; the God of Jacob is our fortress."

Psalm 46:1–7

"The LORD roars from Zion, and utters his voice from Jerusalem, and the heavens and the earth quake. But the LORD is a refuge to his people, a stronghold to the people of Israel."

Joel 3:16

"No temptation has overtaken you that is not common to man. God is faithful, and he will not let you be tempted beyond your ability, but with the temptation he will also provide the way of escape, that you may be able to endure it."

1 Corinthians 10:13

"Let us then with confidence draw near to the throne of grace, that we may receive mercy and find grace to help in time of need."

Hebrews 4:16

So we can **rejoice** ...
in our freedom from sin and death, in
our restored relationship with Him, and
in our future home in heaven.

"Behold, I have given you authority to tread on serpents and scorpions, and over all the power of the enemy, and nothing shall hurt you. Nevertheless, do not rejoice in this, that the spirits are subject to you, but **rejoice that your names are written in heaven.**"
Luke 10:19–20

"Therefore, since we have been justified by faith, we have peace with God through our Lord Jesus Christ. Through him we have also obtained access by faith into this grace in which we stand, and **we rejoice in hope of the glory of God. Not only that, but we rejoice in our sufferings**, knowing that suffering produces endurance, and endurance produces character, and character produces hope, and hope does not put us to shame, because God's love has been poured into our hearts through the Holy Spirit who has been given to us."
Romans 5:1–5

"**Rejoice in the Lord always; again I will say, rejoice.** Let your reasonableness be known to everyone. The Lord is at hand; do not be anxious about anything, but in everything by prayer and supplication with thanksgiving let your requests be made known to God. And the peace of God, which surpasses all understanding, will guard your hearts and your minds in Christ Jesus."
Philippians 4:4–7

"Blessed be the God and Father of our Lord Jesus Christ! According to his great mercy, he has caused us to be born again to a living hope through the resurrection of Jesus Christ from the dead, to an inheritance that is imperishable, undefiled, and unfading, kept in heaven for you, who by God's power are being guarded through faith for a salvation ready to be revealed in the last time. In this you rejoice, though now for a little while, if necessary, you have been grieved by various trials, so that the tested genuineness of your faith—more precious than gold that perishes though it is tested by fire—may be found to result in praise and glory and honor at the revelation of Jesus Christ."

1 Peter 1:3–7

Because God has already won ...
and in Jesus Christ, the victory is ours too.

In case you missed it, that was one awesome sentence:

The Lord reigns, which means He is our refuge, so we can rejoice because God has already won!

"For the LORD your God is he who goes with you to fight for you against your enemies, to give you the victory."
Deuteronomy 20:4

"What then shall we say to these things? If God is for us, who can be against us? He who did not spare his own Son but gave him up for us all, how will he not also with him graciously give us all things? Who shall bring any charge against God's elect? It is God who justifies. Who is to condemn? Christ Jesus is the one who died—more than that, who was raised—who is at the right hand of God, who indeed is interceding for us. Who shall separate us from the love of Christ? Shall tribulation, or distress, or persecution, or famine, or nakedness, or danger, or sword? As it is written: 'For your sake we are being killed all the day long; we are regarded as sheep to be slaughtered.' No, **in all these things we are more than conquerors through him who loved us.**"

Romans 8:31–37

"So we do not lose heart. Though our outer self is wasting away, our inner self is being renewed day by day. **For this light momentary affliction is preparing for us an eternal weight of glory beyond all comparison,** as we look not to the things that are seen but to the things that are unseen. For the things that are seen are transient, but the things that are unseen are eternal."

2 Corinthians 4:16–18

"They will make war on the Lamb, and **the Lamb will conquer them, for he is Lord of lords and King of kings,** and those with him are called and chosen and faithful."

Revelation 17:14

Your Turn

5. In light of the preceding verses, describe God's favor toward those who are persecuted for righteousness' sake.

6. In what ways has God been a refuge for you in times of trouble (even if you've failed to recognize it until this very moment)?

7. What are some specific reasons you have to rejoice, in spite of any difficult circumstances you might currently be facing?

8. Reread Revelation 17:14 from the previous page. How does the King's assured victory help you live out your calling as one of His chosen ones?

EXT. HIGH ROCK (DUSK)

(The sun is about to set. Matthew has fallen asleep among the tablets containing the sermon outline. Sandals on rocky soil. Jesus approaching Matthew. He gently shakes him awake.)

JESUS: Matthew.

(Matthew stirs, then sits up.)

MATTHEW: Yes, Rabbi.

JESUS: I've got it.

MATTHEW *(rubbing his eyes)*: The opening?

JESUS: Yes.

MATTHEW: What is it?

JESUS: A map.

MATTHEW: A what?

JESUS: Directions. Where people should look to find Me.

MATTHEW: Okay, give me a moment.

(Matthew takes a sip of water from a canteen and shakes himself to wakefulness. While Jesus walks to the overlook that views the camp, Matthew grabs his notebook.)

MATTHEW: I'm ready.

(Jesus looks up at the camp. It's quiet.)

MATTHEW (CONT'D): Rabbi?

JESUS *(A pause. And then—)*:

Blessed are the poor in spirit, for theirs is the kingdom of heaven.

(We see Nathanael under the fig tree.)

Blessed are those who mourn, for they shall be comforted.

(We see Andrew grieving the arrest of John the Baptist.)

Blessed are the meek, for they shall inherit the earth.

(We see Little James and Thaddaeus tending the fire.)

Blessed are those who hunger and thirst for righteousness, for they shall be satisfied.

(We see John and Big James right after Jesus named them the Sons of Thunder.)

Blessed are the merciful, for they shall receive mercy.

(We see Mary Mother putting a shawl over Mary Magdalene's uncovered head.)

Blessed are the pure in heart, for they shall see God.

(We see Thomas and Ramah exchange a look at the start of the journey with Jesus.)

Blessed are the peacemakers, for they shall be called sons of God.

(We see Philip diffusing a situation between Simon and Zee.)

And blessed are those who are persecuted for righteousness' sake, for theirs is the kingdom of heaven.

(We see Roman troops arresting John the Baptist.)

Blessed are you when others revile you and persecute you and utter all kinds of evil against you falsely on my account.

(Matthew glances up. A moment of understanding passes between the men.)

JESUS (CONT'D): Rejoice and be glad, for your reward will be great in heaven.

MATTHEW: Yes. But how is it a map?

JESUS: If someone wants to find Me, those are the groups they should look for.

Prayer Focus

Talk to God about the prospect of facing persecution from the world due to your commitment to Jesus. Tell Him about your fears regarding opposition and about any actual occurrences when others have reviled you or persecuted you or uttered evil against you falsely on account of your faith (Matt. 5:11). Thank the Lord that He has chosen you to share in the kingdom of heaven on this side of eternity and that He has given you the Holy Spirit as a Helper in times of trouble. Ask for His Spirit to empower you to hold fast to the truth no matter what comes, to love your enemies and to pray for those who treat you poorly … and to experience *even now* the eternal joys of belonging to His kingdom.

Sample Prayer

Dear Lord,

Your Word says that hardship and opposition are part of what it means to follow Jesus, and I'm actually frightened by the idea. Thank You that nothing can come my way without first being measured out by You, and thank You that You have already provided Your Holy Spirit to be my Helper. Please help me remain faithful to You even when I'm pressured and persecuted by those who (perhaps even unknowingly) oppose the truth of the gospel. Help me to lovingly respond to people, knowing that at one time I too was opposed to You. Thank You for rescuing me. Help me to experience Your joy now as part of Your eternal kingdom.

Amen.

Conclusion

BLESSED ARE THE CHOSEN

In the last episode of season 2 of *The Chosen*, Jesus describes the Beatitudes as a kind of map, saying, "If someone wants to find Me, these are the groups of people they should look for." Of course, the map is simply a sketch since Jesus's chosen followers are hardly perfect in their embodiment of the Beatitudes. His first-century disciples *weren't* perfect, and neither are His twenty-first-century disciples. But that's sort of the point, because Jesus knew what His followers needed to hear:

1. The Encouragement They Longed For

As we mentioned, the eight Beatitudes in Matthew's account of the SOM can be divided into two groups. The first four blessed statements are more *personal* and promise a reversal of fortune for God's chosen people as they continue looking to Him: blessed are the poor in spirit, those who mourn, the meek, and those who seek righteousness, for they will be satisfied and comforted. They will have their place in the land, and they will inherit the very kingdom of God.

So be encouraged, you chosen ones, despite your current circumstances.

2. The Challenge to Reorder Their Priorities

The last four blessed statements are more *interactive* and promise end-times reward to the chosen as they continue to love others well in the midst of life's difficulties: blessed are the merciful, the pure in heart, the peacemakers, and those who suffer for the sake of righteousness, for they will receive mercy and see God and be called His children. They will experience—on this side of eternity!—the kingdom of heaven that is already theirs.

So keep responding to others as Jesus would, you chosen ones, in the midst of your current circumstances.

We are charged with being the hands and feet *and heart* of Jesus to the dying, broken world we still live in, which means responding to and interacting with people in a completely countercultural way—like our Savior does. And by His grace, we'll receive the strength to do it, all the while knowing and holding fast to this:

That as God's chosen people—wholly and dearly loved—we're on our way to an eternal glory that far surpasses our wildest dreams.

Which means congratulations are in order.

God's favor is upon you.

"Blessed be the God and Father of our Lord Jesus Christ, who has blessed us in Christ with every spiritual blessing in the heavenly places, even as he chose us in him before the foundation of the world, that we should be holy and blameless before him. In love he predestined us for adoption to himself as sons through Jesus Christ, according to the purpose of his will, to the praise of his glorious grace, with which he has blessed us in the Beloved."
Ephesians 1:3–6

NOTES

NOTES

NOTES

NOTES

ABOUT THE AUTHORS

Amanda Jenkins is an author, speaker, and mother of four. She has written six books, including *Confessions of a Raging Perfectionist*, a memoir that has inspired women's Bible studies and conferences around the country. She specializes in writing and teaching raw authenticity in our faith, and she is the lead creator for *The Chosen*'s extra content, including *The Chosen* devotionals, volumes I and II, and the children's books *The Chosen: Jesus Loves the Little Children* and *The Shepherd*. She lives just outside of Chicago with her children and husband, Dallas, creator of *The Chosen*.

Dallas Jenkins is a filmmaker, author, speaker, and father of four. Over the past twenty years, he has directed and produced over a dozen films for companies such as Warner Brothers, Lionsgate, Universal Studios, and Hallmark Channel. He is now the creator of *The Chosen*, the first-ever multi-season show about the life of Christ and the highest crowd-funded media project of all-time. He is also the coauthor of the bestselling *Chosen* devotional books.

The official evangelical biblical consultant for *The Chosen* TV series, **Douglas S. Huffman** (PhD, Trinity Evangelical Divinity School) is Professor of New Testament and Associate Dean of Biblical and Theological Studies at Talbot School of Theology (Biola University) in California. Specializing in New Testament Greek, Luke–Acts, and Christian Thought, he is the author of *Verbal Aspect Theory and the Prohibitions in the Greek New Testament* and *The Handy Guide to New Testament Greek*; contributing editor of such books as *God Under Fire: Modern Scholarship Reinvents God, How Then Should We Choose? Three Views on God's Will and Decision Making*, and *Christian Contours: How a Biblical Worldview Shapes the Mind and Heart*; and contributor to several theological journals and reference works. Dr. Huffman can be seen on *The Chosen*'s "Bible Roundtables" on *The Chosen* app. He enjoys working with Biola undergraduate students, pointing them to Scripture as God's Word for us today.